Praise for Orbs:
Their Mission and Messages of Hope

"The phenomenon of the orbs shows us that we are moving in a spiritual dimension that by far exceeds our ordinary perception of the way things are. This field of unlimited potential, which is accessible, friendly, and reliable toward us, becomes visible through the orbs. Klaus and Gundi Heinemann impressively document this with many examples and photos in this book. It opens our eyes."

— **Bert Hellinger,** author, originator of Hellinger Family Constellations, founder of Hellinger Sciencia

"When Anthonie van Leeuwenhoek used the microscope to introduce us to bacteria and microorganisms, he opened another dimension. Now we are being introduced to yet another mysterious dimension, that of the orb. I expect this new experience will yield an even more exciting world than did the microscope. Here you will find unequaled beauty and mystery!"

— **C. Norman Shealy, M.D., Ph.D.,** professor of energy medicine, president emeritus, Holos University Graduate Seminary

"Crystal-clear science, heartful stories, and amazing photos that capture both the mystery and the realness of the orb phenomena. A timely and well-conceived contribution to encourage us all to open to the presence of loving spirits in our lives."

— **Emma Bragdon, Ph.D.,** author of *Spiritual Alliances* and *Kardec's Spiritism,* and producer of documentary films *A Tribute to John of God* and *Spiritism: Bridging Spirituality and Health*

*"Orbs miraculously appear in hundreds of thousands of photos all over the world. In **Orbs: Their Mission and Messages of Hope**, Klaus and Gundi Heinemann present a beautiful symbiosis of the factual and the intuitive. If you are looking for a glimpse into the meaning and messages behind this phenomenon, this is the book to read."*

— **Richard Bartlett, D.C., N.D.**, founder and author of *Matrix Energetics* and *The Physics of Miracles*

*"Who hasn't been delighted when orbs appeared unannounced in their photographs? Yet, in **Orbs: Their Mission and Messages of Hope**, we come to appreciate these phenomena at a much deeper level, recognizing their role in interdimensional communication. Through beautiful photography and touching stories, the authors skillfully evoke within us the mystery of our existence. They suggest it's time to stop asking 'how' and, instead, embrace the opportunity for spiritual evolution that the spirit beings within the orbs, are offering us. An excellent book!"*

— **Christine Page, M.D.**, mystical physician, author, and intuitive

Orbs

Also by Klaus Heinemann

The Orb Project,
by Míċéal Ledwith and Klaus Heinemann

Expanding Perception

Orbs

Their Mission and Messages of Hope

Klaus Heinemann, Ph.D., and Gundi Heinemann

HAY HOUSE, INC.
Carlsbad, California • New York City
London • Sydney • Johannesburg
Vancouver • Hong Kong • New Delhi

Published and distributed in the United States by: Hay House, Inc.: www
.hayhouse.com • *Published and distributed in Australia by:* Hay House
Australia Pty. Ltd.: www.hayhouse.com.au • *Published and distributed
in the United Kingdom by:* Hay House UK, Ltd.: www.hayhouse.co.uk •
Published and distributed in the Republic of South Africa by: Hay House
SA (Pty), Ltd.: www.hayhouse.co.za • *Distributed in Canada by:* Raincoast:
www.raincoast.com • *Published in India by:* Hay House Publishers India:
www.hayhouse.co.in

Interior photos/illustrations: Most images are by the authors, refer to page
127 for other credits

The authors of this book do not dispense medical advice or prescribe
the use of any technique as a form of treatment for physical, emotional, or
medical problems without the advice of a physician, either directly or in-
directly. The intent of the authors is only to offer information of a general
nature to help you in your quest for emotional and spiritual well-being. In
the event you use any of the information in this book for yourself, which
is your constitutional right, the authors and the publisher assume no re-
sponsibility for your actions.

Library of Congress Cataloging-in-Publication Data

Heinemann, Klaus W.
 Orbs : their mission and messages of hope / Klaus Heinemann and Gundi
Heinemann. -- 1st ed.
     p. cm.
 Includes bibliographical references.
 ISBN 978-1-4019-2886-5 (pbk. : alk. paper) 1. Spirit photography. 2.
Orbs. 3. Spirits. I. Heinemann, Gundi, 1942- II. Title.
 BF1381.H45 2010
 133.9'2--dc22
                                    2010015226

Tradepaper ISBN: 978-1-4019-2886-5
Digital ISBN: 978-1-4019-2940-4

13 12 11 10   4 3 2 1
1st edition, October 2010

Printed in the United States of America

*To our children
and grandchildren*

Contents

Foreword

I am honored to write the Foreword for this ground-breaking new book by Klaus and Gundi Heinemann. No words could adequately express my respect for them, not only for their professionalism in presenting the information that will transform lives, but also for the humility with which they approach the subject at hand and the people with whom they live and work. Their integrity in the research and presentation on the consciousness of orbs and their healing intentions is impeccable.

Some of you reading this book may be familiar with the background of Klaus Heinemann, Ph.D., and the books he has authored and co-authored over the past 20 years. You may know that he was a research professor of materials science at Stanford University and is well respected for his lifelong efforts within that field.

While the subject of this book is related to physics in a broad sense, it is not full of scientific formulas that tend to confuse and discourage the stoutest of readers. On the contrary, it is designed to eliminate confusion, provide an elementary and adequate demonstration of the reality of orb consciousness, and offer insight into the orbs' capacity to interact as helpers and healers to those with whom they come into contact.

The Heinemanns' finest hour is revealed in the research and writing of this book. They have traveled the globe photographing orbs in South America, Europe, and the United States. Gundi is a professional in her own right, offering her expertise in the field of energy healing. She has assisted her husband with orb projects since their personal discovery of orbs in 2004. Together they appeared in *Orbs: The Veil Is Lifting* DVD along with seven other professionals, introducing orbs to those of us who are curious about those bright circular objects in our digital photos. Since that time, the mass of evidence recorded by the Heinemanns provides overwhelming proof of the consciousness of orbs and their intentions of healing for our lives.

Judgments about religious orientation, scientific theories, and people in general will not be found between the covers of *Orbs: Their Mission and Messages of Hope.* Neither will you find ghost hunts and haunted houses in the text of these pages. What you will find is a refreshing collection of stories about people discovering orbs, sharing their photos, and becoming keen observers of these phenomena and the meaning orbs bring to their lives. Among these many stories is one of my own—a karmic trip through the life of George Eliot. Beginning with the discovery of an orb in a library photo and culminating in a karmic revelation and healing, my story as well as others' will open your mind to new possibilities for personal and planetary healing. In addition, many of the photos in *Orbs: Their Mission and Messages of Hope* are suitable art forms and may be used as a focus for meditation and healing regardless of one's religious orientation.

New mind/body/spirit authors enter the publication arena daily, meandering through the metaphysical landscape. But now and then, a phenomenal book or two will break through with shocking clarity. Klaus and Gundi Heinemann have written such a book here. Two other names you might recognize as influential writers in this regard are Masaru Emoto (*The Hidden Messages in Water*) and Lynne McTaggart (*The Field*). If we consider the work of these and other cutting-edge writers, we find that their methods of discovery and revelation may vary, but the emphasis of mind, body, and spirit under the single umbrella of consciousness does not.

In 1962, U.S. astronaut John Glenn orbited the earth three times, exceeding speeds of more than 17,000 miles per hour. Fewer than 50 years later, private citizens can reserve a seat on a Russian spacecraft to visit the International Space Station. Progress comes quickly when people embrace a concept and work toward a common goal. It is my fervent belief that the work of Klaus and Gundi Heinemann will be a guiding light to all who are forging new frontiers for the healing of mankind.

— Freda Chaney, D.D.
George Eliot Lives: An Incredible Story of Reincarnation

Introductory Note

Multitudes of people all over the world have been noticing opaque circular features (Photo 1) in their flash photographs taken with digital cameras, making them wonder what they mean. In a previous book, *The Orb Project*,[1] co-authored by Klaus and Dr. Míċéal Ledwith, we examined these phenomena in great detail and presented suggestions about what they might be and how they get captured on the photos.

Reading *The Orb Project* is certainly helpful but is by no means a prerequisite to the understanding of this book. Here we invite you on a journey of discovery and expanding perception, asking if there is a meaning, a relevant message associated with the appearance of these orb phenomena.

Such a process of exploring new terrain can be rather personal. It is like an adventure into a new country you have never visited. Each explorer on this trip has unique experiences, depending on what they see, sense, or feel. May the pictures and stories presented here from numerous orb enthusiasts from around the world fill us with wonder, awe, and amazement. Let us explore what it might mean to us.

This book is in the truest sense a cooperative effort. The authors, a husband-and-wife team, have taken most of the orb pictures and worked on their meaning from day one, at a spiritual retreat in Chicago in the fall of 2004, when the famed healer Ron Roth asked them to take photographs at his intensive. The writing of this book became a joint project, yet facets of it went into directions that were most germane to each of the contributors. Gundi, who is an educator by training, a healing arts practitioner certified in numerous alternative healing modalities, and an artist/photographer, has more intensely focused on the artistic side of this work with orbs. Klaus, who is a physicist by training, has ventured more into aspects that have to do with explanations, rationale, and logic as related to his research efforts on orbs.

Both share a keen interest in religion and spirituality, and it is in this area that their work, as presented in this book, is entirely congruent.

But the difference in academic training does explain why some of the chapters appear more as if they were written by Gundi, while others hint more to the writing style of Klaus. A complete stylistic merging was neither intended nor realistically possible. Nevertheless, the authors are in complete agreement about the material presented in this book, and they have been delighted to work together on it.

Introduction

*The most beautiful thing we can
experience is the mysterious.*

— Albert Einstein

The question of whether there are conscious life-forms outside of our physical realm[1] has been, without question, one of the most discussed and most divisive subjects that mankind has faced throughout its history.

Until very recently, there has only been anecdotal evidence—albeit lots and lots of it—in support of the notion that "nonphysical" life exists. This is because the average person can neither directly see nor sense "other-worldly" life-forms, or devise a physics experiment with which to unquestionably detect them. We have been indoctrinated to think that things that cannot be seen or weighed or detected with conventional scientific methods cannot be real. The subject has been a matter of *belief.*

Consequently, depending on our individual conditioning and personal preference, we find ourselves somewhere between believing or disbelieving in the existence of a nonphysical reality and of nonphysical individualized intelligence and consciousness. We typically find ourselves somewhere on a scale that extends all the way from blindly accepting it, even though unseen, to being fanatically opposed to even entertaining the notion that it might exist.

On the other hand, if nonphysical individualized intelligence and consciousness does exist, the fact that it cannot be sensed or measured suggests that it, or "they," must have a very tough time getting the attention of us humans. Even if we overcome the hurdle of our conditioned skepticism, and entertain the idea that spirit beings might exist, even if we have sincere openness toward them and welcome them as a highly important aspect of reality at large, we have no clear-cut methodology to communicate with them. We cannot unequivocally perceive them, or understand their answer to a question we might be asking, or understand messages they might be trying to send us.[2]

The emergence of orb photography has changed all this. The predominant handicap of Spirit Beings (which is the simplified term we use when we talk about other-worldly individualized carriers of intelligence and consciousness)—getting the attention of mainstream human beings—has been overcome. Making use of digital photography, it appears that Spirit Beings have devised a means to provide irrefutable evidence of their existence, and this evidence is now accessible to anyone, clairvoyant or not, who has a standard point-and-shoot digital camera.[3]

Even though there are still many unanswered questions about the exact imaging mechanism of orbs in our photos, we are fairly certain about the following:[4]

1. Orbs are likely not Spirit Beings in and by themselves, but rather emanations from Spirit Beings.

2. Orbs show up of their own volition in digital photos and sometimes even in photos taken with conventional emulsion film cameras.

3. Due to the technology involved, it takes extremely little physical energy for an orb to be recorded in a digital photograph.

4. Orbs appear to take the minute amount of physical energy required for being recorded in digital images from the camera flash, or in a few cases, from other physical light or energy sources.

5. To minimize the energetic requirement for being recorded by cameras, orbs do not wastefully emit their (light) energy, but instead focus it with laserlike accuracy into the camera rather than into other directions where there is no camera to capture them.

6. Orbs respond to requests to appear in photographs and will generally not bother showing up in photos when they anticipate their presence will not be noticed.

Given this evidence of intelligence/consciousness on the part of the Spirit Beings whose emanations people see in their digital photos, it is reasonable to assume that they do not just appear in images for no particular reason. Instead, we can argue that there is intent behind their showing. The more highly evolved the being, the more likely this assumption is accurate.

Not dissimilar to how it is with beings in the physical realm, we can assume that in the spiritual realm we have a great spectrum of individualized intelligence. There may be beings with a childlike mentality that might simply enjoy being photographed. As they mature, their ability of discernment will mature, and they may choose to show in photos only if there is a particular reason for them to do so. It may well be as simple as that. We typically see many more orbs in our nature photos than in photos taken in settings containing people. This may well be indicative of different types of Spirit Beings present and photographed: low-evolved "nature spirits" will typically show up in nature settings, and beings with higher degrees of consciousness will want to join in the photos taken around people for a specific reason.

In this book, we focus mostly on those orbs that we assume represent emanations from highly evolved Spirit Beings. And of those, we assume that, even though they cannot speak in an audible human fashion, they likely want to communicate something to us when they make themselves visible in photos.

We can then speculate that highly evolved Spirit Beings making their presence known in orb photos will attempt to communicate in any number of ways, including directing a message to the person taking the photograph, delivering a message to the person being photographed, or directing a message to a group of people or even to mankind at large.

Since we can rule out audible recording of messages from orbs,[5] we will have to look in our orb photos for visual messages that are coded by their color, size, intensity, shape, and location, and also by the features that are often recognizable within them (mandalas, missing sections, faces).

It is also conceivable that messages in certain orb photos are intended for communication on a direct-intuitive level. These messages are obtained by contemplation over the photo of an orb, being in a meditative, receptive state and tuned in to your inner perceptivity.

In this book, we report on rational and intuitive evaluation of a large number of orb photos with regard to specific messages that may be contained in them, using these general analysis criteria.

It is not our goal to impress the reader with how wonderful the orb photographs appear. You can find plenty of spectacular orb photos on the Internet. Instead, we often show quite modest pictures of orbs; the kind that you will see in your own photographs, if you set your mind to it. What is magnificent about orbs is not how bright, how large, or how many you capture in one photo, but that they are *there,* and what that means to you. The messages they likely want to convey to you are simple, practical, affirming, and helpful. Tune in.

CHAPTER ONE

AUTHENTICITY OF ORBS

The most pathetic person in the world is someone who has sight but has no vision.

— Helen Keller

HEALTHY SKEPTICISM

At the onset we would like to emphasize that there is a valid and important place for healthy skepticism. We invite skeptics to check our findings, test the grounds, be inspired, and hopefully explore and discover the meaning behind their own orb photographs.

One of Klaus's earliest childhood memories is of his mother telling and reading stories to him. He would ask if it was a "true" story and would refuse to listen unless she confirmed it. This sense of crystallizing the truth and weeding out hearsay has stayed with him ever since. The fruit of that seed continued through graduation with a doctoral degree in physics from a renowned university in Germany, through years of performing research at NASA and Stanford University, through authoring and co-authoring more than 60 peer-reviewed scientific publications in the specialty of materials science, through writing a textbook in solar energy engineering, and through founding and directing (for more than two decades) a corporation performing contract research for NASA. Distinguishing truth from falsehood in engineering and scientific subject areas has indeed always been a high priority for Klaus.

However, with the advent of quantum physics and the theory of relativity about a century ago, everything changed. Physicists have had to expand their view about how the world works, and they had to expand their perception with regard to *how* to arrive at truth. The Newtonian worldview—albeit still valid in all down-to-earth engineering-like subject areas, from building toys to landing a spacecraft on Mars—became outdated. We have learned about the laws of probabilities, quantum changes of state, curved space-time reality, and velocities greater than the speed of light. We have learned about the difference between the brain and the mind and know that the realm of the mind knows no spatial and temporal limits. In fact, we know that the mind is not at all confined to the physical body, and every thought and spoken word anywhere in the universe at any time is still "around" and can be retrieved.

Along with all these changes has come the realization that the method with which we have traditionally separated truth from falsehood is also no longer adequate. The "scientific method" is in need of redefinition. *Reproducibility* of *no-nonsense* experiments, a formerly perfectly logical definition of the scientific method, used for about 400 years, is no longer sufficient.

Science considers as "nonsense" something that is "inherently bad and chaotic"; something that—according to Newtonian physics—is nothing and cannot be seen, weighed, measured, heard, or calculated to exist; and something that is false, irrational, and/or unknowable. This definition of *nonsense* has a built-in cognitive deficit, in that we are defining it with the same term, i.e., that which "makes no sense."

A new, expanded, and contemporary definition of *nonsense* is needed. For example, nonsense might be redefined as "something that is unintelligible and lacks meaning." This new definition would be congruent with modern physics and leaves space, time, and human mental inadequacy out of the equation. We can no longer leave it up to the individual person to determine what is *nonsense* and what is not. Applying this redefinition of *nonsense* to what is unintelligible in the broadest sense, and further qualifying this with whether meaning is present, renders the task of determining what is *nonsense* more objective. Could we still dare to discard evidence like the one shown in Photo 2? (The topic of faces in orbs will be dealt with in detail in a subsequent chapter of this book.)

With this new understanding of *nonsense*, the second traditional criterion of the scientific method, *reproducibility*, becomes—rightfully so—much more difficult to achieve. It used to be that, if an experiment could conceivably be biased by the thought of the experimenter, it would have to be eliminated from consideration as scientific research. All of Professor William Tiller's epochal psycho-energetic experiments[1] would thus fall by the wayside and be categorized as nonsense. So we must consider the possibility that an experiment that is not reproducible, or is not consistently reproducible, is still a valid experiment.

Consequently, our statement that skepticism has an important role in the scientific exploration of new concepts must be qualified with the requirement that the new, broader definition of *nonsense* must be accepted by the skeptic. Without this, no true advance in the understanding of reality is possible.

DUST PARTICLES
OR SPIRIT EMANATIONS?

Now then, are orbs genuine emanations from Spirit Beings, or should they be explained as coincidental photographic defects? This question has been asked ever since orbs were first observed in photographs. We have devoted an entire chapter in *The Orb Project* to this topic.

In spite of this already published support for the authenticity of orbs, Klaus simply cannot justify, as a trained scientist, writing another book on this still controversial phenomenon without at least mentioning why he is convinced of the orbs' authenticity. His current argument on this subject is presented in Appendix B of this book. It is his conclusion, from extensive research in this area, that an overwhelming majority of orb images seen by photographers all over the world are authentic and not caused by camera defects, reflections at airborne particles or moisture droplets, or other diffraction phenomena. Here we touch only on the most important arguments, but we encourage you to peruse the more in-depth discussion in the appendix.

The most prevalent argument presented by critics against the authenticity of orbs is that they are believed to be reflections off airborne particles positioned in close vicinity of the camera's lens. This explanation cannot be upheld for numerous reasons which we explain in Appendix B, including a recent experiment in which an orb was photographed under clean room conditions, i.e., in an environment where airborne particles of the size that could explain reflection effects simply could not have been present.

Other arguments brought forth by some critics center around impurities or abnormalities related to the camera or the electronic recording device built into the camera. This class of arguments can be dismissed with several pertinent facts, including numerous orbs photos taken by the Dutch professional photographer Ed Vos,[2] as well as many others, on conventional photo film.

Yet the most significant argument in favor of the authenticity of orbs is that there is striking, overwhelming evidence that orbs show up in certain strategic photos and strategic positions within a photo. The evidence of strategic appearance and positioning is so convincing that it is all but impossible that *all* incidences of orbs could be rationalized as statistically random and anecdotal. This indicates that orbs are much more than random reflection effects. The nonphysical beings, of which orbs are believed to be emanations, may well use this particular positioning of orbs in photos to try to communicate with the people taking the photos or those seeing or studying them. Much of what we present in this book is devoted to this subject.

THE "EVEN IF" RATIONALE

Even if all orbs in our photos could be proven to be nothing other than normal physical reflections of the flash at airborne particles, it could still be argued that the mere circumstance that we see these orbs in photos and positions that are clearly not random indicates that thought from outside of our physical realm may be involved.

The argument would then shift from explaining the origin of these orbs to how the placement of these airborne particles can be so strategic. How can it happen that these physical airborne particles are, in that very moment when the flash is triggered (and with respect to the very position the camera is held), arranged into the highly defined constellation that leads to meaningful positioning of the orb in the resulting photograph?

Airborne particles should always be in statistically random locations; the orbs would then have to be expected to show up in photos only at statistically random locations—almost *never* in "meaningful" positions.

So even if reflection at airborne particles were the origin of these orbs, and I am not at all saying that this may in fact be the mechanism, the mysticism about evidence of nonhuman thought would be undiminished.[3] It would shift from the "miracle" of producing (a tiny amount of) physical energy with means from another realm to the undiminished miracle of affecting the positioning *and* timing of numerous tiny airborne particles in a meaningful way that clearly defies the laws of statistics.

It is our position, then, that since orbs appear in meaningful places in photographs, and not haphazardly, it is because they are there by design.

ENERGETIC CONSIDERATIONS

What is really happening when we take photographic pictures of orbs? The fact that orbs show up in photos indicates that some form of physical process is at work. So, what is it?

As we hypothesize on the basis of the evidence at hand, the process begins with the consciousness of a sentient being outside of this world and ends as physical evidence on the image of a recording device. In other words, an intentional energetic imprint from a reality *outside* of our physical reality is recorded *inside* of our physical reality.

Even in the event that we eventually do learn to fully understand how this comes about, i.e., how orbs get recorded in our cameras—and we do not doubt that we will eventually improve on this understanding—this will simply mean that we will have understood one of two steps of the entire process, but not the entirety of the process.

Another step would be to learn how these sentient beings are able to "produce" the physical energy that is clearly required for this recording process. The actual amount of physical energy required to produce an image of an orb in a photo is extremely small, perhaps no more than the energy which is contained in 1,000 photons,[4] i.e., a very, very tiny amount of energy. Fathom this: the energy would be about one-billionth of one-billionth of the amount of energy required to keep a conventional 100-watt lightbulb lit for one second.

But nevertheless, even though tiny, it is energy, and it does indicate that the reality in which these non-physical beings reside has an energetic component. It also shows that these beings have succeeded in taking advantage of a human technological achievement that converts the tiniest amount of energy into something that is visible and demonstrable. The conversion of a tiny bit of photon energy becomes a large, bright, and sometimes colorful, photographic recording that we can see and enjoy over and over again. This is remarkable!

The process used to create this energy is not yet understood, because we don't understand the reality of these beings. They may be able to convert energy, such as from an electronic flash, or they may produce the energy themselves, and then focus it toward the recording device. In such a case, they can then conserve precious energy by not aiming it into directions where it's not needed or won't be discovered, i.e., where there is no camera.[5]

There are clearly many unanswered questions about the physical aspects of orb photography. The essence of this book is to explore the orbs' mission and the messages they are trying to communicate.

CHAPTER TWO

ORBS AS TRANSFORMING SYMBOLS

*When we quit thinking primarily about ourselves,
and our own self-preservation, we undergo a
truly heroic transformation of consciousness.*

— Joseph Campbell

From a physics point of view one could argue that an orb is likely some sort of plasma-like energetic feature. The laws of thermodynamics suggest that the energetically most favorable shape of nonsolid agglomerates is a sphere, which, of course, becomes a circle in the two-dimensional projection of its photographic image.

It is, therefore, no surprise that the evidence is overwhelming that the circular shape of the orbs in most orb photos is actually a projection from spheres and not from disks. If the latter were the case, we should see plenty of elliptically shaped orbs, which is contrary to hundreds of thousands of orb photographs from all over the world.

The sphere and the circle are the most basic shapes in physics and mathematics. They have no beginning and no end and no clearly defined direction. They have perfect symmetry. They look like an integrated whole. While the circular shape suggests that orbs are actually quite ordinary, circles and spheres have always had a special influence on the human psyche. Take a moment and look around in your home. How many things do you have that have a circular shape? For example, just from our writing desk, we can see two spherical lamp shades, three spherical tea lights, four chairs with circular backrests, a candle holder with eight round inserts, a globe, several cylindrical candles, a fabric batik wall covering with hundreds of interspersed circles, four circular stained-glass art pieces, a cylindrical drum, a spherical chalice, and dozens more round or circular items, and of course, our circular wristwatches and wedding bands. It is as if we are magically attracted by this basic circular shape. It has become a powerful, pervasive symbol.

The attraction of the spherical or round shape of orbs does not only come from its pleasant periphery, but quite frequently also from what is inside. Rarely are they just filled with uniform, gray contrast. Most often they show intriguing interior features.

In this chapter we will first take a look at the transforming power orbs can have when we look at them under high magnification. We will then discuss round-shaped symbols, including mandalas, in some more detail and deduce what important message for people might be understood as conveyed by certain orbs.

MESSAGES BY DIRECT INTUITIVE KNOWING

*There are no extra pieces in the universe. Everyone
is here because he or she has a place to fill, and every
piece must fit itself into the big jigsaw puzzle.*

— DEEPAK CHOPRA

Much more than most of us would probably admit,
we humans are wired to perceive on an intuitive level.
Direct intuitive knowing plays a key role in most of our
day-to-day action and decision making. We are drawn to
one book in the bookstore but not another. We instantly
feel attracted to one particular person but want no interaction with another. Sometimes we sense what a person
is about to say, even before she has spoken the first word.

Similarly, certain transforming symbols have a profound influence on us; they give us guidance on our
path through life. Some speak to us in such subtle ways
that we hardly notice they are present.

Certain classes of orbs may have such a transforming
effect on us. The general beauty or mystical features of
their appearance, their geometric yet random shapes—
with irregularities that seem to make no sense and leave
much room for imagination and interpretation—stim-
ulate our underdeveloped intuitive perception. Are we
seeing a face . . . or two? Is it an angel? Perhaps a guardian angel? Is a deceased loved one visiting?

We don't know for sure. The mere fact of not knowing may be what has a magical effect on us. Our mind
is incredibly powerful. Placebos have cured more people
than all medication combined, including cancer, blood
pressure, and pain.[1] If our minds derive such power from
simple chemical pills, how much more power could we

possibly derive from viewing a beautiful image originating from a conscious and even a very highly evolved being from a reality other than our own?

We invite you to look at the orb in Photo 3. Take it in, ponder it, and allow it to speak to you. Make a note of the first thoughts or insights that spontaneously come to you, as they might be significant keys for you at this moment.

Do the same, in a playful way, with Photo 4 and imagine that you are connected to some highly evolved, benevolent being from the Spirit realm. It has the best intentions for you and is there to help you. Try it again at another time, when you are ready to receive a new message.

These transforming symbols can also have a direct healing effect on you. As you connect with the Spirit Entity whose emanation you are looking at, you will likely intuit some meaningful answers for the next step to be taken and even receive desired healing. Openly enjoy this new adventure; repeat it as often as you wish.

You might wonder about the brown segments in the lower right corner of Photo 4. It is actually the top of a wooden triangle, which is used as a transforming symbol at the Casa de Dom Inácio, in Abadiânia, Brazil, home of the famous healer João de Teixeira de Fario (known as "João de Deo" or "John of God" or simply "Medium João"). People coming to the Casa meditate in front of the triangle and leave pictures and healing intentions and requests for loved ones, if they so choose.

A triangle has been considered for ages as a metaphor for the feminine and the masculine, seen as principles, reaching up to the divine. The triangle is a powerful symbol often used to express stability. Its baseline represents mankind's rootedness in the earth. The two sides reaching up express the human desire for more, as we reach into the realm of the unknown, the field of unlimited potential.

It so happened that this powerful symbol, the triangle, was standing on the altar at a healing retreat held by Ron Roth in Chicago, Illinois, where we had been invited to take pictures. One of the most beautiful orbs we ever photographed (see Photo 4) placed itself at the top of this triangle, as if to say, "Hey, pay attention! There is some significant meaning for you to discover from here on forward."

Two clairvoyant friends independently identified that orb, as well as the orb in Photo 2, as key ascended masters known in the Judeo-Christian tradition. Take this into consideration when you contemplate these two photos again. Open up to the intrinsically positive, the beautiful, the unconditional love emanating from these spiritual greats.

THE MESSAGE FROM ORBS AS TRANSFORMING SYMBOLS

Symbols come to us and speak in their unique language that directly communicates to the soul. They have transforming abilities. Symbols point toward something that allows us to change and move forward toward what is essential. They are like signposts on the way, pointing toward deeper meaning and what brings significance in our life.

Symbols speak to our intuitive way of taking in data. They reach directly to our core, circumventing the mind in communicating information.

The circle, or the sphere in a three-dimensional expression, represents oneness, wholeness, unity—"come-unity," coming together as one.

When they saw the Earth as a sphere circling in space, the astronauts had a profound experience. The pictures of the globe on which we all live, taken from the moon in 1968, became a transforming symbol to remind us of our interconnectedness and the fragile state of the system on which we all live. Photos of planet Earth, now readily available to be seen by everybody, serve as a reminder of our destiny to come together as one.

Digital photography makes it possible to see things that heretofore could not be seen. People in many places around the world report having taken photos of circular light phenomena, or orbs, which we have identified as emanations from Spirit Beings, conscious entities that are not part of our physical world.

Perhaps their visibility is intended to wake us up to the following notions:

1. You are one

2. All is one

3. We are one

4. One Earth, one humanity, one spirit

5. One people, interconnected, interrelated, with one destiny

It becomes clear that only by working together we can solve our numerous global challenges.

No wonder that orbs show up in great numbers when people celebrate, sing, dance, and do things together in a joyful, cooperative way. Perhaps they want to remind us of our true purpose, to realize come-unity as we live in harmony and work together for the benefit of all.

The orbs serve as powerful reminders of our destiny. When these light spheres are photographically enhanced and enlarged, an intricate interiority with intriguing shapes and different colors becomes visible. They have symbolic significance. It is likely that specific messages expressed in these features will become clear in time.

Freddy Silva, one of the world's foremost experts on crop circles and orbs, recently stated that the orbs seem to replace the phenomenon of crop circles. In principle, all phenomena tend to be ignored or rationalized away by some critics. With the abundance of orbs, being captured by thousands of people like you and us all over the world, where enjoying photography with a digital camera is essentially the only required common denominator, we seem to receive strong signals to pay attention to what connects us all.

Ignoring these signals is becoming increasingly difficult and, at the same time, irresponsible. In the process of coming together, cooperating for the benefit of the whole, wonderful possibilities can unfold. As we anchor the idea of "all is one" deep in our hearts, we can release our innate gifts and co-create life in a conscious, fulfilling way with magnificent global outcomes.

The messengers of hope are around us, waiting to help—they have always been, but now we can actually see them. They live in an energetically different system, and their entanglement with our robust physical system has heretofore been too subtle to be recognized by us humans. Our mainstream technological achievements and advances in science have not helped, but actually aggravated our ability to connect with other realms, until the digital camera made it possible for us to receive "their" messages on a large scale.

Orbs have become so powerful that it is getting harder and harder to ignore them. They show nothing new, but they communicate in a fresh way the wisdom that has always been there. May we, the human species, become perceptive to this wisdom! Let's explore what that wisdom may be.

CHAPTER THREE

MESSAGES BASED ON LOCATION

Those things that nature denied to human sight, she revealed to the eyes of the soul.

— **Ovid,** *Metmorphoses*

The placement of genuine orbs within photographs often appears not to be random, but instead, strategically positioned. In this chapter we present several typical examples of this very significant observation and attempt to interpret the likely, or possible, intent behind the specific locations. In most cases, we believe the intent is related to the circumstance under which the photograph was obtained, including nonphysical considerations, such as the thoughts, emotions, and feelings of the person taking the photo or being photographed. We therefore add the relevant stories to the photos we are presenting. (Throughout the book, names are occasionally changed to preserve the privacy of individual contributors.)

MARKING OUR HOTEL ROOM

Orbs can communicate surprisingly specific messages by presenting themselves in certain locations in a photo, when the detailed circumstances of the photo and photographer are included in the assessment.

Klaus had just completed a two-hour live radio interview on orbs by phone from our hotel room at the La Fonda Hotel in Santa Fe, New Mexico. The interview went very well. As is our practice during the frequent radio interviews, Gundi was nearby, helping by focusing on and intending for the highest and best outcome of the interview. We both felt a Presence directing the interview. The spoken words flowed naturally and just the right examples and stories appeared on the "inner screen" of Klaus's mind to be brought forward for the listeners. When the interview was over, we decided to get some fresh air and walk around the hotel. Gundi got the idea of taking a picture, imagining and inviting our invisible helpers from the interview to show up in the photo near our room. The picture (Photo 5) shows a bright orb and an equal-sized orb of lower intensity marking precisely our hotel room!

The statistical probability of this occurring—two orbs marking the room in which we had held the interview—is quite low indeed. We intentionally took only one photo of the event, so as not to water down the result.

From the photo we cautiously concluded that Spirit Beings generally want to communicate, and that they are able and willing to answer our request, be it to show themselves in a specific location or to assist us when we ask for help.

On a more personal note, we further concluded that they wanted to tell us that they were happy to have helped in the radio interview. We took their message as an affirmation that our positive feeling about the interview was accurate. We also took from their appearance that we can rely on their help when we ask for it, and that their mode of helping is through intuition. All we need to do to accept their help is to get out of the way and let the intuition come through, just as Klaus had done during the interview. Because he is typically operating from a dominant left-brain perspective, feeling secure and at ease with right-brain notions was both powerful and unusual for him.

PRESENCE AT THE WEDDING

A heartening message was presented during a dance at the wedding pictured in Photo 6. The person who took the photo reported: "I have experienced a kundalini spiritual awakening due to the physical death of my 18-year-old son. This photo was taken at my daughter's wedding a year later. I remember watching my daughter and her husband dancing and feeling so blessed and loved that this was happening. I also was thinking about my son, knowing that he was present."

Looking at where the orb placed itself in the photo, one would be tempted to read into it a very positive response to the photographer, perhaps something like, "Yes, mother, I *am* present, and I am very happy with you and my sister, and all is well! Do not worry! Enjoy!"

FAREWELL PARTY?

The person who sent us Photo 7 supplied the following narrative: "[... the orb] is huge and stands just above the head of a person who died four months later. She was a dear friend of mine."

She then described that the photo was taken at the occasion of her 50th birthday party.

This picture was taken in a sequence with several others; only this one shows this huge orb. I appear in red in the picture, and the orb seems to stand just above the lady in the green jacket (Carola). I know exactly what I was thinking and feeling at the time. I was deeply happy and grateful to the universe to have this little birthday party, after a painful end of a relationship. Carola was the one who organized the party. We were very close friends. The context is psychological, but it is a very special one: the energy between Carola and me. The fact that, a few weeks later, she collapsed again with a cancer she had been living with for four years makes this even more significant. She died four months after the picture was taken. I keep on wondering if that orb . . . could have been some kind of angel who was protecting her, since she was terrified about death, and I was the one who had been trying to tame it for her for years.

So, when the picture was taken, I was in pure joy and gratefulness about this gift of friendship. The picture was taken just after the candles on the cake had been blown out. Everyone is very happy.

Analysis reveals that the orb is real. It is actually closest to (actually hovering right above) Carola. This can be determined from the depth of focus in the image, the circumstance that the camera was focused on Carola, and digital analysis done on the photo.

The message intended to be communicated with this orb photo is likely of a personal nature, intended for the persons photographed. Their joyous state of being at the time the photo was taken may have prompted a benevolent being from the Spirit world to let them know that Carola's impending passing would be into another realm, not into nothingness.

THE BEST B&B TO SPEND THE NIGHT?

Stop knocking on the door: You're already inside!

— RICHARD ROHR

We made lodging arrangements in advance by Internet for our trip to the southern U.K. When we arrived at our B & B in the rural village of Zennor in Cornwall, we were taken aback by the misrepresentation of amenities listed on the residence's Website. While we were preparing to leave to look for another inn for the night, we took a picture of the charming 260-year-old typical Cornwall living room with fireplace (Photo 8). Immediately we discovered a small, bright orb beaming at us, as if to say, "Hey, you've got to stay here!"

We did stay, and the landlady made us immediately feel at home with her authentic, generous, and nurturing attitude. It was a beautiful experience; the place turned out to be absolutely perfect for us. We had interpreted the message of the orb correctly.

THANKING THE SINGER

Beauty saves. Beauty heals. Beauty motivates.
Beauty unites. Beauty returns us to our origins,
and here lies the ultimate act of saving . . .

— MATTHEW FOX

The gifted African-American singer Renee had just given a mesmerizing performance during the service of the famed theologian and healer Ron Roth, who put his arm around her and thanked her for her heartfelt singing. In Photo 9 the Spirit Being whose emanation showed up seemed to be stating, "Yes, we agree! It was marvelous and, after all, we are singing through you!" The singer herself humbly acknowledged something to this extent when we showed her the photo.

ENGAGEMENT AT THE WATERFALL

I hold this to be the highest task for a bond between two people:
that each should stand guard over the solitude of the other.

— RAINER MARIA RILKE

Orbs are often easy to overlook in a strongly textured background. We have, therefore, applied contrast enhancing digital processing to Photo 10. There were two people and two orbs positioned so they would be detectable in the photo, despite the highly textured background. The orbs in this photo seem to bring a message of joy and support in this very special time of decision! This picture was taken only moments after this couple had agreed to spend the rest of their lives together. And the presence of the orbs shows that they believe this couple is well suited. The couple is happy about our interpretation that representatives from another dimension seem to be pleased with their decision.

THE SPIRIT GUIDE

Love is our true destiny. We do not find the meaning of life by ourselves alone—we find it with another.

— THOMAS MERTON

When Gundi took Photo 11, she stated that she had followed a clear hunch to photograph that scene at that very instant. It shows a friend, Dana Duryea, left, who is executive director of the Foundation for Spiritual Development in San Rafael, California, in consultation with a friend. Without hesitation, when he first saw the photo, Dana, who has a very astute awareness of the presence of Spirit Beings, stated, "This is one of my Spirit Teaching Guides."

Seen or not seen, such presence of Spirit Guides may well be the norm, rather than the exception, even if every photograph doesn't reveal them. This ought to humble us when it comes to claiming originality of our ideas, since there seem to be Spirit Beings around us to assist us every step of the way. As if to underline that there is no doubt about Dana's statement, the Spirit Emanation is shown in movement, which is one of the preeminent indications that the orb is genuine.

THE HEALINGS RECORD BOOK

*I firmly believe that all human beings have access
to extraordinary energies and powers. Judging from
accounts of mystical experience, heightened creativity,
or exceptional performance by athletes and artists,
we harbor a greater life than we know.*

— JEAN HOUSTON

After they received an invisible intervention at the Casa de Dom Inácio, the recipients recorded their names and addresses into a record book. In Photo 12, an orb is hovering precisely over that book, as if to remind people that there are larger forces at work helping to heal.

THE SKEPTICAL STEWARD

The captain of a cruise ship was giving his welcoming address to the passengers (Photo 13), and it was evident that a Spirit Being had an interest in what was going on and agreed with what he was saying. His address resonated deeply with us. The captain very thoughtfully acknowledged the international crew, committed to excellent service and demonstrating a spirit of oneness and harmony for travelers who had come together from many continents. "If we can get along here on this small floating island, we can do it everywhere." The captain pointed out that the key is not so much what kind of ship we use: large or small, metal or wood, "no matter where we are going and whatever vessel we have chosen, what's important is to focus on *relation*-ships."

After we took the picture, our steward noticed our astonishment. We explained that an emanation of a Spirit

Being had positioned itself near the captain's head. "No way," he exclaimed. "That's impossible!" We showed him the photo, but he was unconvinced.

So we left it at that. Nevertheless, we could not help but take a photo of him when he came to our table to serve the festive dessert. When he saw Photo 14 with an orb above his head, he became an instant orb enthusiast. The orb was in this photo as if to say, "Hey look! We're really here. Believe in us." The whole crew showed a great interest in orb photos thereafter. The orb had brightened the "life in a day" of several crew members. Many more scenes with bright orbs presented themselves during the remainder of our voyage.

THE LEANING BAPTISTRY

When you change the way you look
at things, the things to look at change.

— MAX PLANCK

It was a rainy afternoon in Pisa, Italy, with only occasional dry periods. We took photos as our tour guide was explaining the significance of the statue of the Mother Mary and baby Jesus above the entrance of the Battistero, which is a separate building next to the cathedral with the famous Leaning Tower. An orb showed up near the Holy Mother in the picture taken at that very moment (Photo 15). Then the tour guide diverted our attention to a subject more interesting to her: she said that the Baptismal leans—not quite as much as the Bell Tower, but still clearly distinguishable. Take a look at the photo and see for whom this part of the story is less interesting! No orb shows in the photo taken while the guide talks about the *leaning* Battistero.

PADRE PIO

> *Pray, hope, and don't worry. Worry is useless.*
> *God is merciful and will hear your prayer.*
>
> — SAINT PIO OF PIETRELCINA

It filled us with awe to experience the place where Padre Pio had worked. The small hospital he initiated decades ago had grown into a huge medical facility, still expanding and providing work for large numbers of people with a variety of skills.

Numerous visitors come year-round as pilgrims to San Giovanni Rotondo in southeastern Italy to pay respect to the famous Padre Pio da Pietrelcina who was beatified by John Paul II on May 2, 1999. When walking around the Padre's sarcophagus, there was no doubt that his presence was felt in the room. Like many other spectators, we dared to take a quick photo (Photo 16) of the area and immediately, as expected, a bright, moving orb showed up on the photo screen. Padre Pio's spirit was still bringing guidance and support to his followers.

THE SKEPTIC'S ORB

> *There is freedom only when there*
> *is freedom from the known.*
>
> — KRISHNAMURTI

Hindelang, in the Allgäu region in southern Germany, is a spectacular place to gather family and friends for a celebration. The panorama of mountains invited us to sit for hours and watch the changing night sky in front of us and take some photos (Photo 17). One of Gundi's rather skeptical brothers was still questioning the authenticity of orbs. The orbs in this photo we had just taken would not convince him.

He jokingly said, "Just point your camera to the left, to the hill from which we can hear the cow bells, and take a photo!"

Gundi followed his instructions and took a photo of scenery we had missed earlier (Photo 18). Surprise! The brightest orb seen during that particular evening showed up in the photo. Another skeptic was converted.

GRADUATION

Every word or concept, clear as it may seem
to be, has only a limited range of applicability.

— WERNER HEISENBERG

John sent us this picture (Photo 19) taken by a class-mate during his graduation from hypnotherapy school.

Not only was there one very bright, moving orb but numerous smaller congratulants from an unseen realm showed their presence in the picture also. John, the person in the middle, noted that an orb had placed itself beneath his certificate (Photo 20), stating: "At the time of receiving my diploma, I felt that hypnotherapy and its specific teachings 'connected the dots' in my three-year study of complementary healing arts!"

Is the orb located near the seal of the certificate telling John, who is already a highly accomplished person with several post-graduate academic degrees, that the seal of approval has been bestowed onto him and he should now *apply* this art of healing service? Is it telling him that the invisible world will be assisting? Is the bright, moving Spirit emanation a specific helper to the teacher and to the faculty at large, telling them that they are being assisted in their endeavor to teach the art of complementary healing? And are the other "visitors" seen faintly in the picture at the ceiling, curtain, and door more members of the "advisory faculty in the spirit world," each expressing their happiness that, once again, a group of graduates has gained the wisdom they are so eager for us to acquire so we can create a better world for all? It is plausible.

While the classmate who took the picture has been an astute orb photographer, it appears that we are seeing here an example of an orb photo where the message is primarily directed at the person(s) photographed, as well as at a specific segment of the general public beyond that (the faculty of the school).

PREPARING FOR THE TRIATHLON

To dare is to lose one's footing momentarily.
Not to dare is to lose oneself.

— SOREN KIERKEGAARD

Three orbs found their way into this photo (Photo 21) of two women getting ready for a triathlon. This year, Kristin, right, is joining them in the event as first-time participant. Connie, left, confided that their expectations for protection and successful outcome of this unusual and challenging event are high. The photo assures them that their wishes have been heard and guides from the invisible realm are present to protect them on their adventure.

The orbs are located at areas of focus for this exercise—the heart and the quads. The message of the orbs thus appears to be individualized and directed at the people in the photograph.

ORBS AT THE DRUID CEREMONY SITE

How wonderful that we have met with a paradox.
Now we have some hope making progress.

— NIELS BOHR

In this remote meadow, we were waiting for the sun to go down so we could take numerous photos for one of our orb studies. A young reporter—still new and somewhat skeptical of the orb phenomenon at large—had joined us for the event. He had placed his tripod under one of the huge oak trees on the side of the circular meadow site and was hoping to catch some orb photos once the sun had set.

Looking at the photographer's ready-to-go camera under the oak tree, Gundi felt called to take a photo from where she was standing (Photo 22). A noticeable bright orb placed itself right in front of the waiting camera on the grass as if to say, "Of course, we are here with you, ready to be photographed, just don't be timid. It is somewhat amusing to us that you all take so many photos and welcome us with such enthusiasm. Trust, we are surrounding you at all times!"

WITH GOD ALL THINGS ARE POSSIBLE

When the higher flows into the lower, it transforms
the nature of the lower into that of the higher.

— MEISTER ECKHART

There was a spiritual healing event at a large church in Palo Alto, California. The literal writing on the wall could not have been any clearer: "With God all things are possible!" An orb confirmed this statement by placing itself under "all things" (Photo 23).

In preparation for this healing service, we had placed a few symbols on the altar that were out of the ordinary, including a globe next to the altar candles as if to request the healing of nations.

The beings of light from the invisible realm seemed to have registered the intentions. One seems to have placed itself right over the Middle East on the globe (Photo 24) as if to say, "We are doing our best. The rest is up to you humans. Act on the quotation of one of the world's greatest teachers, 'With God all things are possible.'"

THE PHOTO SESSION

The newspaper article written by Hazel Courteney about orbs for the feature "A Life in the Day: Klaus Heinemann" was ready for printing by the Sunday *Times* in London.[1] Only an up-to-date photo of Klaus was missing for the orb story. It was contracted to be produced by a professional photographer at our home in California. We wondered if orbs would show up on demand for such a project, in particular when taken with a professional camera not ideal for orb photography (likely one with a CMOS image sensor). Somewhat doubtful but still optimistic, just prior to the arrival of the photographer, Gundi took 15 photos of Klaus sitting in his chair looking at *The Orb Project* book. In 12 of the photos taken, orbs showed up near Klaus's head and upper body (Photo 25). This seemed to indicate to us that the Spirit orbs were communicating: "the newspaper story is important to us."

CHAPTER FOUR

GENERAL MESSAGES

Everything science has taught me—and continues to teach me—strengthens my belief in the continuity of our spiritual existence after death. Nothing disappears without a trace.

— **Wernher von Braun**

FIREWORKS ON SAN ANTONIO DAY

Italians live with their saints and honor them like special family members. When we were in Vieste, southeastern Italy, we had the privilege of experiencing Saint Anthony's birthday celebration (Photo 26). A parade through town with a trumpet concert in the marketplace and spectacular fireworks lighting the night's sky marked the event. We watched it from our hotel room and were happily surprised that numerous spheres of light (orbs) joined in the celebration as if to affirm, "Yes, we saints live on among you; thank you for acknowledging us."

33

WORKING FOR THE UNITY
AND WELL-BEING OF ALL

*Each of us can manifest the properties of a field of
consciousness that transcends space, time, and linear causality.*

— STANISLAV GROF

Like two bright lights in the night sky, orbs seem to
highlight the above message.

At the Second International "Orbs: Interacting with
Other Realms" Prophets Conference at Palm Springs,
California, in 2008, a conference participant took a
remarkable photo (Photo 27) during our presentation,
which we had entitled "We Are Surrounded by a Cloud of
Witnesses."[1] The photo shows two large and very bright
orbs on either side of us. The text of the slide shown at
the moment when the picture was taken reads: "It is in
every one of us to be wise and to work cooperatively for
unity and the well-being of all."

During the presentation, we both strongly felt the
presence of guides (one each) from another realm with
the message that the orbs are here to be with us and to
help us. The bright orbs clearly highlight the message
that, as we tune into our inner wisdom, we will find ways
to work cooperatively for the unity and well-being of all.

When we first saw the photo, there was little doubt
in our minds that the two large orbs, placing us in between them, represent an answer from our guides, telling
us that they agree with what we conveyed in our presentation. This message, in a nutshell, was that orbs are emanations from Spirit Beings and convey to humanity that
they love us and are there to assist us in the necessary leap
in consciousness of humanity at large that is required to
preserve our planet for future generations.

But does this interpretation concur with Linda Horton, the person who took the photo? When we asked Ms. Horton to address this question, she said, "Your photo was a precious, beautiful gift for you and for me. I only know I had a huge burst within myself and the directive to shoot that picture."

A very large number of orbs were present earlier, during the beginning of the same PowerPoint presentation. Photo 27 is representative of many photos taken by various conference participants during our talk. In this type of photo, the positioning of the orbs is less significant than their quantity, because of the attempt of the Spirit Entities to spread out their orb-emanations so that all of them could be seen, rather than by specific positions in the scene. Perhaps the great number of orbs showing up is indicative of their support of the topic.

Note also the variety of orb types present, ranging from bright circular orbs with little or no discernable interior features to orbs with interior "eyes," irregular exterior boundaries, and different colors. One might even be tempted to see faces in several of these imaged beings, such as in the green entity above the flower arrangement left in the photo.

ME, TOO!

At another conference on orbs, a participant took Photo 29, again showing numerous orbs during our presentation. A particularly bright one apparently desires to be included in the circle of orbs shown in the particular slide we were discussing. It adapted quite well to the size of the orbs in that slide. Clairvoyants identified the orb as a very highly evolved Spirit Being.

CHAPTER FIVE

ORBS AROUND CHILDREN

Your children are not your children. They are the sons and daughters of Life's longing for itself.

— Kahlil Gibran

It is expressed in the teachings of many religious and spiritual traditions that in the spiritual realm particular interest and concern exist for children. They are helpless and have to cope with masses of impressions in the new environment into which they were born, but they have not yet acquired the intellect to deal with all of this.

Children are still in touch with their natural intuition and allow themselves to be guided by it. In fact, numerous published records show that children have a much higher tendency to actually see Spirit Beings. When we are open and receptive and listen to children, we hear them talk about light beings, angels, or balls of light (orbs). Sometimes we even hear children talk to these beings of light. These phenomena are simply part of how they see reality, and it comes as a great surprise to them when we say that we cannot see the Spirit Beings.

37

In some cultures, such as those that are prevalent in the Philippines and Brazil, parents are aware of this tendency in children and support it by their own understanding. In most Western cultures, however, adults are skeptical about these phenomena, and, as they communicate their doubts, the children in time begin to doubt themselves. Since they want to fit in, they begin to ignore their unique gift of perception and eventually lose it. They will actually stop seeing Spirit Beings altogether, sooner rather than later.

Many stories and orb photographers from around the world document that Spirit Beings are abundantly around children. We have a hunch they are there to assist them and protect them in numerous ways. Perhaps also their playful exuberance and joy, as well as their adventurousness and curiosity, attract them. In this chapter we bring a few examples.

MOUNTAIN LIONS

You must not allow yourself to dwell for a single
moment on any kind of negative thought.

— EMMET FOX

If there are any doubts that the old saying about children being surrounded by their guardian angels is true, this story may help dispel those doubts.

A few years ago, we facilitated a christening ceremony for our daughter-in-law Annabel's three daughters. We held the ceremony in a beautiful nature preserve near San Francisco. About a year after the ceremony, Lorraine, a family friend and mother of two girls in the same age range, hiked with the girls in that same area. That is where Photo 30 was taken.

About it, Annabel wrote: "This photo was taken by my friend Lorraine who took the girls on a hike in Edgewood Park up to that lookout point where we had our little ceremony with the girls! I warned her to keep an eye out for mountain lions since there had been a number of sightings reported. She hadn't heard about them, and, at first, she thought I was joking. She called me from the lookout to see if I was serious and I said yes, so she was a little worried with four little kids running around on the trails! Looks like she had some company keeping them safe!"

DANCING GIRLS

Perhaps inspired by the piano in the background, three-year-old Vaila and five-year-old Isabella enjoyed showing off their latest twists and turns learned in recent ballet classes. Their own laughter and happy expressions provided the sound track. No wonder that a big orb above Vaila's head (Photo 31) joined in this unique expression of joy and happiness.

Dressing up and dancing in colorful clothing is another favorite pastime for preschoolers. The orb in Photo 32, attached to Krista's hat, participates in the fun experience.

BIRTHDAY PARTY AT U-TUBE

Laughing kids were coming down huge plastic slides and having great fun (Photo 33). It seemed impossible to keep track of our granddaughters in the midst of the giggling, climbing, and sliding pile of friends. The group photo taken of the happy crowd at the end of the afternoon showed an orb right above the youngest girl. We wondered and were a little concerned how hearing-impaired, two-year-old Krista would manage in such a lively group event. It seems her "guardian" was watching and staying close to her all the time.

Note also how appropriately the orb selected a perfect spot in this busy scenery, so it could be easily spotted: on the only uniform, relatively dark-colored feature in the entire picture. Perhaps the red area below, right above Krista's head, would have also been an effective location, but then, Spirits have their preferences, too. Choosing the color blue as a background may have been part of their message. Blue is commonly associated with trust, loyalty, wisdom, confidence, intelligence, faith, and truth. The message may be that beings from the unseen world will be around our children and consistently help, protect, and guide them.

MIRACLE ON A TRICYCLE

Life is divine, life is an extraordinary, incredible,
miraculous phenomenon, our most precious gift.

— ROBERT MULLER

Little Krista, here just two years old, is determined to get the most out of life in spite of having come to this world with serious physical challenges. Her athletic sisters and parents include her in all the adventures that bring them joy. In Photo 34, Krista delights in practicing her turns on her pink tricycle—on the day when her new cochlear implants were turned on and, for the first time in her life, she could hear. The orb in her tow seems to indicate that she is protected and guided from benevolent Spirit Beings of the invisible realm, and that they are joyous about the new aspect in her life that is now unfolding.

FIFTH-GRADE SCHOOL PERFORMANCE

When I approach a child, he inspires in me two sentiments: tenderness for what he is, and respect for what he may become.

— LOUIS PASTEUR

Our daughter invited us to her fifth-grade class's school theater performance. Seated in the back of the multipurpose room at the elementary school where our daughter Connie was teaching, we took some photos of the performance. Many of the photos unexpectedly contained orbs. A year later, there was a literal repeat performance when Connie took the pictures herself! Again, friendly guardian angels marked their presence (Photo 35).

ICE SKATING

Numerous emanations from Spirit Beings appeared in many pictures we took at an ice skating event for children. We have circled some of the fainter ones so they can be seen more easily (Photo 36). We can detect just about one visible orb for each child in the rink.

CHAPTER SIX

ORBS AROUND CHARISMATIC PEOPLE

I could be whatever I wanted to be
if I trusted that music, that song, that
vibration of God that was inside of me.

— Shirley MacLaine

SCIENCE AND CONSCIOUSNESS

The effect of multiple orbs showing up in pictures taken at consciousness-raising conferences was replicated numerous times with various speakers. For example, we photographed several keynote presenters at the Tenth International Conference on Science and Consciousness in Santa Fe, New Mexico, in 2008, deliberately taking only one or very few photos of each speaker whom we selected to photograph.

Without prejudice, the results indicate that beings from the unseen reality were *not* equally interested in all presentations! They seemed to strongly resonate with certain topics or presentations, and not show up at all for others. As one example for strong resonance, we show Dr. Rupert Sheldrake (Photo 37) at the end of his presentation on his concept of "morphic resonance." The Spirit Beings present seem to communicate that they agree with his hypothesis that human consciousness is located entirely outside of the human body, in a ubiquitous morphic field, and that it can be accessed by anybody, anywhere, through a resonance detection and amplification process. Particularly poignant is the bright orb with a mandala-like interiority located above the photo of the Earth, as if to say, "Yes, once humanity has understood this paradigm shift in understanding of the nature of consciousness, the future of your planet will be safeguarded."

At the same conference, host Greg Tamblyn provided musical interludes to lighten up the audience (Photo 38). Numerous orbs showed up around him. Note, in particular, a bright representative from another dimension near his hand playing the guitar, as if saying, "Yes, you are playing this instrument well, and we like it!"

Another presentation that drew a crowd of beings from another dimension was by J.J. and Desiree Hurtak, who gave a dazzling presentation on symbolism. (J.J. Hurtak is the author of the *The Book of Knowledge: The Keys of Enoch*.) Listeners from another dimension were everywhere (Photo 39), lining up in front of the dark stage curtain, where they knew they could best be seen.

At the 2009 Conference on Science and Consciousness, Onye Onyemaechi gave a spirited presentation on "Healing through Music, Drumming, and Dance" (Photo 40). Numerous listeners Onyemaechi couldn't see with the naked eye joined in during his healing service, as if agreeing with his approach.

ABRAHAM

Jerry and Esther Hicks are renowned for presentations to large audiences where Esther channels the "Abraham group" of nonphysical entities of "infinite intelligence." At two different meeting series (Photo 41), one year apart, we took one photo each during the preparation phase of their presentation, about five minutes before the session began. Numerous beings from another reality were present in each image. Noteworthy is not only that each photo includes two bright, large orbs, but also that, upon close examination, these two respective sets of orbs appear to have very similar, mandala-like interiorities which may signify that at both events the same Spirit Beings were present.

DEVA PREMAL

I don't know what happens to me on stage.
Something else seems to take over.

— MARIA CALLAS

The famous singer Deva Premal gave a presentation at Grace Cathedral in San Francisco. We took a few pictures at this event from the back of the church (Photo 42). All showed numerous orbs (in unusual size and color variations), indicating that beings from beyond also enjoyed her performance. The orbs gave the impression that they were lined up in a formation pointing toward the big star at the stage where the singer performed.

CHAPTER SEVEN

ORBS AT EPOCHAL EVENTS

Be the change you wish to see in the world.

— Mahatma Gandhi

ELECTION OF A NEW PRESIDENT

Ladies and Gentlemen, I take office at a time in which the world is living in extreme contradictions.

— GUSTAV HEINEMANN (1899–1976, FORMER PRESIDENT OF GERMANY)

Finally the numbers were in, and it was clear that Barack Obama would be the 44th President of the United States of America.

We were gathered in the living room at our children's house to witness this historic event. When President-elect Obama gave his profound acceptance speech, in which he humbly appealed to each citizen, "Together we can make a difference," an orb showed up near him in the TV (Photo 43) not once, but twice in successive photos we took. Perhaps the orb was saying that help is assured as long as we each are willing to do our part in bringing the necessary changes about. To run a country is not a one-man job. It is all of us working together for the larger good that will bring about desired change.

THE HARRY RATHBUN
MEMORIAL PRESENTATION

> *Society as a whole can benefit immeasurably from a climate in which all persons . . . have the opportunity to earn respect, responsibility, advancement, and remuneration based on ability.*

— SANDRA DAY O'CONNOR (MEMBER, SUPREME COURT OF THE UNITED STATES, 1981–2006)

Dr. Harry Rathbun, a revered former Stanford University law professor and spiritual teacher, was being honored at Stanford Memorial Church in Palo Alto in 2007. Professor Rathbun, who died in 1989, was known for his exceptional speeches to graduating students, in which he reminded them of the First and Second Commandments of Jesus of Nazareth as guiding principles for a fulfilled life. During the memorial presentation, former U.S. Supreme Court Justice Sandra Day O'Connor, who had happened to be one of Dr. Rathbun's former law students, gave a moving speech reminding the audience of these principles as guidelines for living. The event was filmed, and no photos were allowed.

We waited until Justice O'Connor and Richard Rathbun, Harry's son, had left the stage, then we took one quick photo while leaving Stanford Chapel (Photo 44). The abundance of orbs captured in this spontaneous last-minute photo tells that many more were present during this history-making, inspirational event than those people fortunate enough to have obtained an admission ticket. Everyone in the audience, including a large number of new Stanford students were able to catch a glimpse of Dr. Harry Rathbun's spiritual legacy, which is well documented in his book *Creative Initiative* and vividly demonstrated by his exemplary life service to those of us who had the privilege to know him.[1]

CHAPTER EIGHT

ORBS AT SACRED PLACES

There are only two ways to live your life:
one is as though nothing is a miracle,
and the other is as though
everything is a miracle.

— Albert Einstein

THE CHALICE WELL

At the occasion of the 2008 Prophets Conference on Orbs: Interacting with Other Realms, we visited this beautiful garden in the heart of Glastonbury, U.K., located at the foot of the famous Tor. The garden includes the Chalice Well, which marks the site where Joseph of Arimathea is believed to have placed the chalice that had caught the drops of Christ's blood at the Crucifixion. Christian mythology also suggests that the red of the water represents the rusty iron nails used at the Crucifixion.

The photo of this little pool below the well shows quite unusual orbs (Photo 45). Two fast-moving opaque orbs presented themselves just in time for this photo, shown in large magnification. The length of streaks with which orbs appear in photos can be used to estimate their speed of motion. The streak of the centrally located orb is several feet long and indicates a speed of approximately 5,000 miles per hour. The orb on the right moved at about 300 miles per hour. The orbs seem to indicate that speed is not an issue when it comes to being present to provide healing assistance.

The water flowing into this pool arranged in the symbolic infinity sign is said to have special healing powers. It has been hypothesized that Spirit Beings are here not only to provide hope but also to physically assist in healing. Their healing ability is believed to be related to their extremely high mobility. See Chapter 12, Spiritual Healing for a more complete explanation of this concept. Might the appearance of two orbs moving at very high velocity yet slowly enough to "see" their motion (Photo 45) give credence to this hypothesis of a subtle energy healing mechanism?

"IF"

We stepped into a small church in the southwestern tip of England, near Mount Saint Michael, and were happily surprised to find in the gift shop a copy of this shortened version of the poem, "If" by Rudyard Kipling:

If you can keep your head when all about you
Are losing theirs and blaming it on you,
If you can trust yourself when all men doubt you,
But make allowance for their doubting, too;
If you can wait and not be tired by waiting,
Or being lied about, don't deal in lies,
Or being hated, don't give way to hating,
And yet don't look too good or talk too wise;

If you can dream—and not make dreams your master;
If you can think—and not make thoughts your aim;
If you can meet with triumph and disaster
And treat those two imposters just the same;

If you can make one heap of all your winnings
And risk it on one turn of pitch-and-toss,
And lose, and start again at your beginnings
And never breathe a word about your loss;

If you can talk with crowds and keep your virtue,
Or walk with kings—nor lose the common touch,
If neither foes nor loving friends can hurt you,
If all men count with you, but none too much;
If you can fill the unforgiving minute
With sixty seconds' worth of distance run,
Yours is the Earth and everything that's in it,
And—which is more—you'll be a Man, my son!

The poem, in this form, was often quoted by Harry
Rathbun, and it had become an unforgettable teaching
for those who heard his legendary commencement addresses. Our discovery of this poem in that small church
at the far end of England sparked our interest and made

us even more appreciative of this relatively unassuming place of worship. We took a photo and were delighted to see two orbs show up (Photo 46), as if to say, "There was a reason for you to enter here. Yes, this poem is worth being taken to heart!"

CHAPTER NINE

ORBS
AT HOME

*Your sacred space is where you
can find yourself again and again.*

—Joseph Campbell

THE PIANO

*Look within. Be still. Free from fear and
attachment, Know the sweet joy of the way.*

— BUDDHA

We both used to love to play the piano but, due to
much distraction and other activities in our lives, we
have not kept up practicing and enjoying this art for several years. At numerous recent occasions we have seen
orbs near our piano (Photo 47). Is there a subtle message
for us to pick up playing this instrument again? We had
quit playing the piano, so our skills are a bit rusty. Are
the orbs telling us that it is not needed to be perfect in
order to enjoy playing a musical instrument? Are they
making us aware that, if we balance work and fun activ-
ity, we will further our well-being?

ANGELS AND ORBS

The orb in this festive scene (Photo 48) of angel ornaments on our coffee table placed itself in the window above a nativity scene and next to several orb-like hanging ornaments, as if to say, "I fit quite well into this scene—after all, I am an angel, too!" Might it also want to say that it is quite beneficial for us to decorate the house with beautiful ornaments, that they might help balance our often hectic lives?

THE RIGHT DECISION?

Since orbs are sentient beings, we can ask them to indicate to us their recommendation to questions we have. They will respond in their own way; the interpretation of the answer is up to us.

The person who took Photo 49 had purchased this residence, which is located in the town where Medium João de Deo works in Brazil. She was wondering if she had made the right decision. The positive response from the world beyond was overwhelming. Just to confirm the authenticity of the photo and eliminate airborne particles as an explanation for the orbs, the pictures she took immediately before and immediately after this photo, within a few seconds, showed no orbs.

BIRTHDAY 101

And in the end, it's not the years in your
life that count. It's the life in your years.

— ABRAHAM LINCOLN

How many centenarians do you know? It's a real privilege for us to know one such person who recently celebrated her 101st birthday and is still, with remarkable sharpness, recalling events in her life dating back almost one entire century. In Photo 50 she is shown, on the right, talking to a person just a few years her "junior." Her daughter-in-law, who took the photo, comments:

The two ladies were laughing and reminiscing about their lives. Both have wonderful senses of humor and outgoing personalities! It was the first time they had met each other, but they had a ball, and celebrated by having an afternoon social drink together. Both of the ladies had several family members present, and they talked about joyful, memorable family happenings. The room was filled with laughter.

—and, apparently, with about as many listeners from another dimension as their respectable ages indicate.

THE PASSIONATE FLUTIST

We are kept from the experience of Spirit, because
our inner world is cluttered with past traumas . . .
As we begin to clear away this clutter, the energy of
divine light and love begins to flow through our beings.

— THOMAS KEATING

A woman who had just read *The Orb Project* sent us Photo 51. It is quite astonishing.[1] The photo contains two very large orbs, in places that suggest a location-related message, as well as a number of other "conventional" orbs that appear to be randomly distributed in the image. In addition—and this is quite unusual—there is a large quantity of distinct tiny orbs that are hard to spot without strong image enlargement. An example is shown in the two section photos below, both equally enlarged. These tiny orbs all have a strong "eye" in the center, but otherwise don't appear similar. They all have individualized internal features.

Amy, the person featured in the picture, is playing an Irish penny whistle. She is a talented, accomplished musician. She has been playing violin since she was five and taught herself the penny whistle about two years ago. She loves old music such as Celtic, Irish, and Medieval. Since her early childhood, Amy has experienced memory flashbacks from what appears to be previous lifetimes. She states:

> When the picture was taken, I was reminded of another lifetime when I believe I lived in Ireland. I got images of rolling green hills and was having fun playing Irish jigs and reels. I remember playing on

the tabletops of my father's pub, with lots of people gathered around me, dancing and clapping.

Was she visited by spirits of some of these people? Was there a general interest in the penny whistle by the beings from the unseen reality, or were they drawn by her performance skills?

> I think they are spirits that love my music! I've noticed, when I play lively, happy songs, I have quite an audience! When I play melancholic, sad, slow songs there are hardly any orbs.

The photo appears to confirm what she intuitively perceives.

ORBS NEAR PETS

Many pet owners have seen orbs in photographs near their pets. From the numerous pictures and stories sent to us, we selected a very unusual one taken by Sandra Sanders (Photo 52). She took this photo in the late 1990s with a conventional throwaway emulsion film camera. It shows her new puppy and an older dog. They had been playing for a while and suddenly stopped and started barking, at which time Susan took a series of pictures, including this one. This series was the only one that showed "shaft" orbs, which are fast-moving orbs leaving a mostly opaque shaft of light. In this particular example, the shaft either originates at, or ends at, the head of her older dog.

Sandra describes the unusual circumstances:

> [W]hen this photo was taken . . . I felt it was a spiritual phenomenon that might have to do with my dad. After my dad recently died, our phone rang constantly and when my husband or I would answer there was no voice, no static, no sound of any kind, no dial tone, nothing, just silence.

This story has several interesting aspects. First, it appears to be a clear indication that, under certain conditions, orbs also choose to show up in regular, conventional emulsion film photos. Second, the story regarding Susan's deceased father may be an authentic attempt on his part to get in touch with Susan and impart a message. Orbs being electromagnetic manifestations may well have the energy to trigger low-power electronic events, such as the "phone calls" Susan is reporting. This is congruent with similar experiences reported by other people, and it is congruent with the strength of the signal evidenced in Susan's photos. Such clear orbs in motion recorded on regular film must have been more energetic than "regular" orbs recorded in digital photos.

Susan was the only person to receive her father's messages. To understand the communication, she may need to include the unusual circumstances into the equation: i.e., the dog and puppy, the highly energetic Spirit emanations during a time when "orbs" were virtually unknown, her late father's profession, the timing, the location, and other "strange" occurrences she might have experienced. Using her intuition as a guide, and assuming that the message and the entire experience were positive, benevolent, and loving, she may receive healing benefits from the Spirit orb messages.

CHAPTER TEN

FACIAL FEATURES IN ORBS

*Transformation literally means
going beyond your form.*

— **Dr. Wayne W. Dyer**

For the longest time, Klaus would not concede that orbs can credibly contain facial features, considering reports of this coincidental and anecdotal.

However, since it was always clear that the Spirit Beings from which orbs emanate are highly intelligent, he would concede that while he had not personally seen any such credible evidence, that it couldn't be *entirely* ruled out. It may, in fact, be possible. Nor would he categorically rule out that other people, who do interpret certain facial expressions into orb images, may be onto something.

Let us now go into more depth with examples of "faces in orbs" that entirely changed his view on this subject.

THE FACES OF JANICE'S ORBS

Photo 53 was sent to us by a British orb enthusiast. We cropped the two orbs from impeccable original photos.

Janice, a London police officer, describes the circumstances of the left photo:

> I would first like to make it clear that I am a very grounded, sensible person. On August 30th I flew to Croatia, where my daughter was going to be married. During the flight I read your article in the *Times* about orbs. I found it very interesting and kept the article to show to a friend. On September 2nd, after the wedding ceremony in the ruined grounds of an old church and the subsequent meal and speeches, we were all led behind an old building which had an open-air dance area backed up by woods—all very rustic and unpretentious—lovely. Just as the music started, I turned my Sony digital camera around to the woods where there was no light source, and before I took a photograph, I remembered your article about the orbs and something you mentioned about inviting the orbs along. I lightheartedly, but quietly said something like, 'If there are any orbs here you are very welcome to join the party.' I then took my picture and was astonished to find an abundance of orbs in it, all of various sizes. I zoomed in to get a closer look at the patterns in the orbs, but one very small one stood out from the others as having a very clear face in it. I did not recall you mentioning the orbs having faces in your article. I was astonished. I zoomed in further to get a closer look, and there is, without

any doubt, a very clear face of some sort of being—
not human—peering out of the orb, just slightly to
its left. You can see the shape of the head, sculp-
tured cheek bones, detailed eyes—quite large eyes,
and a little mouth that appears to be blowing—
even though it may just have a small mouth. It is as
if it is viewing the celebration going on.

Janice also sent a photo taken when she was back
home in London. It contained a tiny orb, shown cropped
and in a high magnification. She commented: "There is
clearly a white face of another being in an orb type object in the [picture]. This to me appears more as though
a little circular portion of the atmosphere has peeled
back to reveal him."

The message from both orbs may be intended for the
photographer who recognizes the features, rather than
for the general public. The first may be a confirmation
to Janice that what she had read about orbs is true: you
can call them in, and they show up in your photo, they
are intelligent, and they are interested in what is going
on around you. The message from the second may simply be to show her that, even though the resolution of
features in orbs is obviously quite low, there is plenty of
possibility for variety of appearance.

The point is not that every reader clearly interprets
the picture the same way as Janice does. There is no absolute right or wrong when it comes to the interpretation
of features in orbs. There remains a degree of subjectiv-
ity on the part of the observer.

FACE IN THE SHED

Trust yourself. You know more than you think you do.

— BENJAMIN SPOCK

Klaus's skepticism for face identification in orb images remained strong—until one evening in late June 2008, when everything changed. Following a presentation on orbs we had given at a conference in northern Germany, the conference organizer invited some of the participants to join them for an orb photography experience that evening in a remote field that was said to be "frequently visited by Spirit Beings." Not being particularly agreeable to the idea that Spirit Beings might like to "hang out" more at some places than others, in particular in remote areas, we reluctantly followed the invitation. In fact, as it happened, the "yield" of orbs in our photos that evening seemed no greater than what we would normally see in our typical, people-oriented settings.

One of the fellow orb photographers, local to the area, suggested that we take a photo of the inside of a deserted shed at the edge of the field. It was completely open on one side. Perhaps decades ago, this shed may have served as a refuge for hikers in inclement weather. The very first shot yielded the Photo 54. Not only did it reveal two very bright orbs, but one of them (note the enlargement of the left orb) contains facial features with such clarity that Klaus's skepticism regarding faces in orbs had no further place to go. No longer was the question *is it possible to see facial features in orbs*, but rather, *whom are we seeing in this photo?*

We then took several other photos of the same scene, so we would be able to analyze this unusual appearance of a Spirit Being with a face and might, perhaps, be able to correlate the facial features (eyes, mouth, mustache, and nose) with "random, real" features in the knotted wooden background. The impact of background features underneath the opaque orb is actually a reasonable argument advanced by skeptics with regard to faces in orbs. Skeptics would argue that the faces seen in orbs are not actually features of the orb itself, but rather come from the features of the background showing through the opaque orb.

See the two pictures showing a zoomed section from the reference picture, as well as the exact same area taken from a subsequent photo (a "control photo") that does not show orbs in this location. We have marked circles in the control photo where the orbs were located in the original photo.

Analysis of the two photos reveals that the eyes on the orb with a face do not precisely correspond to knots in the wood, but they do occur in an area where the wood is strongly darkened. The nose and the mouth do, to some degree, follow certain features in the wood. However, by no means are the features in the control photo so detailed that a face, or facial features, might easily be recognizable.

In the orb on the right side, not the one showing facial features, we find that there are similarly strong background variations in the control photo in the location where the orb appeared, yet this orb shows no indication of facial features whatsoever.

With due caution we conclude from these findings and others similar to them that orbs—or rather the

Spirit Beings from which the orbs emanate—*may* be able to take advantage of physical background features in the image to end up with the appearance of facial images, if that is what they want to communicate.

Further, we conclude from this photo sequence:

1. The main message is primarily directed at the photographer and conveys that orbs can indeed show facial features.

2. Facial expressions can be enhanced by intelligent use of background features, i.e., by intelligent positioning of the orbs in the photo to optimally use these background structures such that the actual overall physical energy required to produce the orb image remains very, very small.

3. Most orb images do not normally show facial features, because the mechanism to produce them is quite intricate and, due to the structure of the background in general, it is often impossible to apply it in every orb photo. For example, orbs on a uniformly colored background will not be able to use this mechanism at all.

4. And finally, without following hunches, neither this photo nor the personalized messages contained in it would have come about. Just as the very first orb we saw in a photo had to be huge and as bright as a lightbulb to attract our attention, the

first facial feature in an orb that would
turn around my preconception had to be
infallibly clear.

THE MILL ON THE FLOSS

These findings were tested with a communication
and photos we received from a person whose story was
outright astonishing. Freda Chaney submitted the following record of orbs she had photographed in her library:[1]

I enlarged the orb on the computer screen and
saw that it seemed to be hovering over a novel, *The
Mill on the Floss* by George Eliot (Photo 55). That
intrigued me, so I enlarged the photo on the screen
even more, and found, in the orb, the faces of a
woman and a young girl. The woman had blonde
hair and a light dress, and the young girl had dark
hair and a dark dress with a white collar.

To satiate my curiosity, I pulled *The Mill on the
Floss* from the shelf and perused it. Inside the book
are paintings of the characters—among them, a
woman with blonde fluffy hair wearing a light colored dress, and a young girl with dark hair wearing
a dark dress with white lace collar. Coincidence?
My husband suggested I should read the book to
see if it held the answer to some mystery in my
own life . . .

The three images (Photos 55 and the two left ones in
Photo 56) are the original photo of the library wall, and
two successive enlargements of the orb and its interior
features. We applied minor contrast enhancement only
to the super-enlargement (lower left in Photo 56).

We must admit that we have a hard time interpreting the details with which Freda described the two women in the orb, but there is little doubt that we can distinguish two beings that appear to be female inside that orb.

We asked Freda to also send us the photo she had taken eight seconds prior to the one that showed the orb on that book. As expected, it did not show an orb in the same location as the first one. Therefore, we expected to be able to analyze the background behind the orb in the first photo to ascertain if there were features that would resemble the facial features in the orb, similar to our analysis of the left orb in the shed in the previous section.

After careful examination of the exact area in which the orb had appeared, using similar contrast enhancement to what we had used to maximize the appearance of the beings inside the orb photo, we came to the conclusion that, with a high degree of confidence, there is no obvious correlation of the background features with the image of the two beings in the orb. This control photo is shown in Photo 56 to the right of the photo with the orb in the same magnification, depicting the exact same segment of the image of the library detail. There may still be some sort of coincidental effect that may have contributed to the impression that there are two beings inside the orb in the left photo, but this "conventional" argument stands on uncertain grounds: the image of the two beings, as faint as it may be, appears to be genuine.

This would then mean that the assumption made in the earlier example, that Spirit Beings, if they want to show up in orbs with facial-like features, make intelligent use of existing background features, may be valid in some but probably not in all cases. They may also simply be able to fabricate, on their own, the image impression they want to convey to the viewer.

We communicated this preliminary conclusion to Freda and recommended that she follow her husband's suggestion to read *The Mill on the Floss,* to perhaps find some clues about the message the orb might be intending to impart to her.

She did, and her first response was, "This is incredible!"

It is evident that George Eliot based the character Maggie in *The Mill on the Floss* on her own life.

"There are so many parallels between Maggie (and George Eliot) and me," Freda wrote, "that it would take much time to record them all. I will list the most obvious ones below. I offer these because I am intrigued by the 'clues' within the book which bring me to understand myself and my own life in a mirrored, objective way."[2]

Freda went on to describe an astonishingly large number of parallels between Maggie and herself—everything from their shared interests, to their common family life, and to their emotional makeup. Here we list only a few:

> "George Eliot studied Divinity, and I graduated with a doctoral degree in Divinity.
>
> "Maggie's brother receives parental preference. My brothers were given preferential treatment by our parents.
>
> "In the end, Maggie dies in a boat, rescuing her brother Tom (who had, for years, rejected her in her adult life). I was nearly killed in a boat when I was out rowing with friends. And, like Maggie, I was rejected by one of my brothers during my adult life.

"I have made some unfortunate choices in the past, and have suffered greatly for it. Maggie did the same. We both have had our 'dark nights of the soul.' We both grew from the experiences, and remained loyal to our sensitivities. Maggie was intensely emotional—so much so that others couldn't understand her. She had a deep desire to be loved and accepted. I lost my mother when I was young, and suffered from lack of nurturing. George Eliot's mother died when she was a teenager, leaving her with emotional setbacks during her lifetime.

"George Eliot married a man named John Walter Cross when her first 'husband,' George Lewes, had passed away. My first husband's name was John Walter."

Freda also mentioned other, even more startling similarities, which she discusses in depth in her book, *George Eliot Lives: An Incredible Story of Reincarnation*. She reemphasizes, "Please understand that I'd never before read *The Mill on the Floss* and only opened the cover because the orb led me there. As a matter of fact, the book was inside its case where the embossed book cover could not be seen sitting on the shelf."

Freda summarizes what she learned from this experience, provided to her through the orb picture:

George Eliot's life and work, particularly *The Mill on the Floss,* have led me to understand that I am not alone in my concerns about being and feeling different among peers. Maggie is a prime example of someone who appreciates aspects of life the way children do—mystically. She is high-spirited and misunderstood as a child and as an adult—something I had struggled with for years. Finally and most importantly, the meaning that was brought to me through Eliot's book is that if we persevere, we will find what we've really always known—that "God writes straight with a crooked finger." If we can survive the dark nights of the soul, we can move on with new meaning into new directions for our lives. We must remain open.

As if these phenomenal similarities between Freda, Maggie, and George Eliot were not sufficient to impress even the starkest critic of orbs and what their message can be, Freda continued to report:

> I also learned that Eliot wrote a novella titled *The Lifted Veil,* a book in which she writes about the paranormal. The bulk of her work speaks of realism. I find it uncanny that she wrote a novella about the paranormal with a title very similar to the title of the DVD *Orbs: The Veil Is Lifting.*[3]
>
> Perhaps, George Eliot has something more to share than the synchronicities between our lives and work. Perhaps the Spirit orb knew how tenacious I would be in researching this information, and that I would share it with others? Could it be a well-laid plan of revelation for the greater good? I know this for sure, I was not interested in her work prior to the orb, so there was little if any chance of my having researched her life and work without the clues the orb offered me.

After all these revelations had transpired, we asked Freda if she had any other photos with orbs she could send us. She selected two from a large repertoire of photos. They had been taken about four years prior to the one with the orb on *The Mill on the Floss*.

Only one of the two is shown (Photo 57). It depicts, in two magnifications, a seating arrangement on her patio—with two orbs "sitting" in an empty chair. The second photo shows an empty settee, with an orb sitting on it.

Why would Freda choose these two pictures from hundreds of orb photos she had in electronic storage? First one seat with two orbs; then two seats with one orb—could this have been a truly random choice? From Freda's perspective, it may have been. But could it be that there is a story behind it?

Here is the story that we cautiously entertain as underlying these remarkable photos and events, told in the form of a hypothesis. The reader may determine if it seems plausible:

George Eliot, fully conscious that Freda is her reincarnation, felt a pressing need to communicate with her. However, Freda was entirely unaware of these communication attempts.

Eliot knew that Freda had become interested in orbs, so she tried to communicate through orb emanations. Two orbs in one empty chair? And then one orb in two empty chairs? Perhaps, she might have hoped Freda would get the clue that the orbs represented two incarnations of soul—that they were still connected in a karmic sense, albeit through one current life—Freda's. But Freda did not make the connection, and Eliot's attempts failed.

Then, about four years later, another possibility for communication emerged, and Eliot immediately pursued it. One needs to understand in this context that, from the perspective where Eliot is, time has little relevance. That reality is essentially timeless. Past is present is future—it's a concept very hard to understand from a human perspective. This time, Freda was taking photos in her library, and the moment presented itself for Eliot to leave an undeniable clue on her own book— an orb which would draw Freda's attention to the book and, hence, to the parallels of their lives. This time, as revealed in this *The Mill on the Floss* story, it worked; Freda noticed the orb and did with it what Eliot had intended.

Freda's story is a prime example that orbs containing facial images are trying to communicate with the person taking the photos. If the Spirit Beings devising the orbs know that the primary person seeing the photo, i.e., presumably the photographer, is perceptive to seeing humanlike facial features, they can, and will, choose to appear in this way. Freda had such perceptivity. Other people might not be as perceptive to that particular avenue of communication by orbs. They might respond much easier through other characteristics of orb images, such as mandala-like interiorities.

Obviously, agreement among viewers regarding certain features in orbs is not what really matters. The key is that we develop our perception to the extent that we understand that there is meaning behind the orb images. The entities from which orbs are emanations will adjust to that and choose the form most fit to the circumstances.

Orbs
Photos

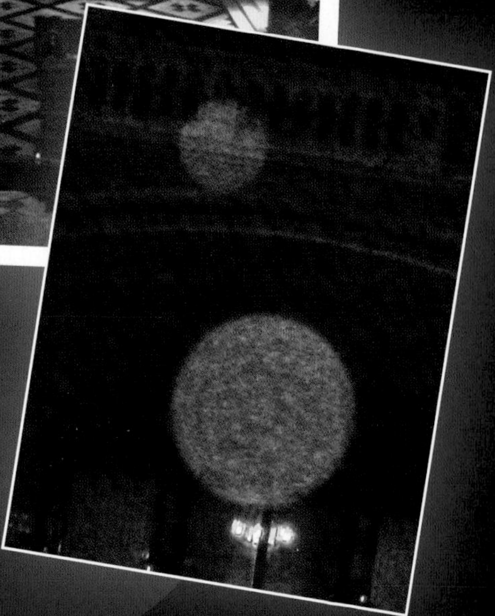

INTRODUCTORY NOTE
Photo 1: An orb with beautiful, colorful interiority in a cathedral, in competition with a stained glass window?

HEALTHY SKEPTICISM
Photo 2: Can we still uphold that seeing faces in orbs is nonsense?

MESSAGES BY DIRECT INTUITIVE KNOWING

Photo 3: An emanation from a very highly evolved Spirit Being, suggested as an example for pondering and allowing a direct-intuitive experience from a realm beyond ours.

Photo 4: An emanation from a highly evolved Spirit Being, attached to the top of a wooden triangle of the type used as transforming symbols at the Casa de Dom Inácio, home of João de Deo in Abadiânia, Brazil.

MARKING OUR HOTEL ROOM

Photo 5: Two orbs mark the hotel room where we had just given a two-hour radio interview.

PRESENCE AT THE WEDDING
Photo 6: Delightful presence from another dimension, with a heartening message to the mother of the bride.

FAREWELL PARTY?
Photo 7: An unannounced visitor at a birthday party.

THE BEST B&B TO SPEND THE NIGHT?
Photo 8: Helping with the decision to stay in a 260-year old B&B in Cornwall, U.K.

THANKING THE SINGER
Photo 9: Thanking a singer; an orb, positioned at just the perfect location, seems to agree.

ENGAGEMENT AT THE WATERFALL

Photo 10: Engagement by the waterfall. Two orbs find a good location in the busy background from where they can "announce their joy" over the accepted proposal.

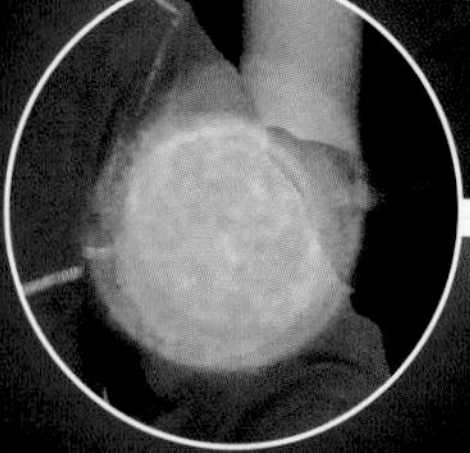

THE SPIRIT GUIDE
Photo 11: Advisor in a consultation?

THE HEALINGS RECORD BOOK
Photo 12: Filling out a "treatment form" after receiving an invisible intervention by João de Deo at the Casa de Dom Inácio in Abadiânia, Brazil.

THE SKEPTICAL STEWARD
Photo 13: The captain's address: ". . . the most important ships are *relation*-ships." An orb likes it!

Photo 14: After initial skepticism when we showed him Photo 13, the steward became an instant "orb enthusiast" when we showed him this picture, taken a few minutes later.

THE LEANING BAPTISTRY
Photos 15: The Leaning Baptistery of Pisa: an orb redefines what is "interesting."

PADRE PIO
Photo 16: Padre Pio's sarcophagus in San Giovanni Rotondo, Italy. An orb moves into the picture above a group of nuns reading a Mass.

THE SKEPTIC'S ORB

Photo 17: From a hotel balcony in Hindelang, Germany. One bright, and several weak, orbs show their presence. The skeptic is not convinced, yet . . .

Photo 18: . . . until, on his request, we shot this picture toward the left of us, and a bright orb appeared in it.

GRADUATION

Photo 19: An orb at the graduation ceremony tries to voice its opinion.

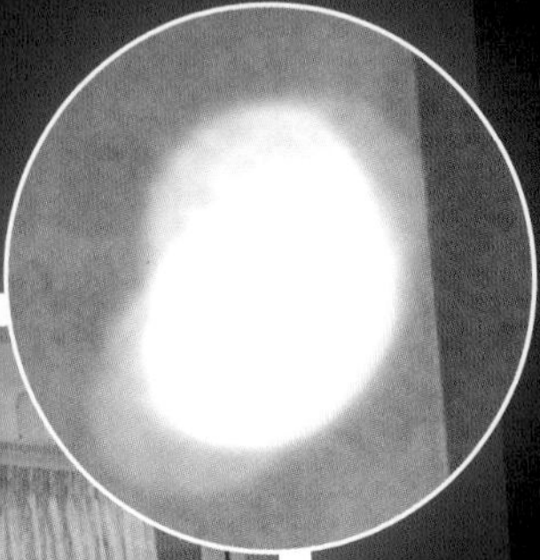

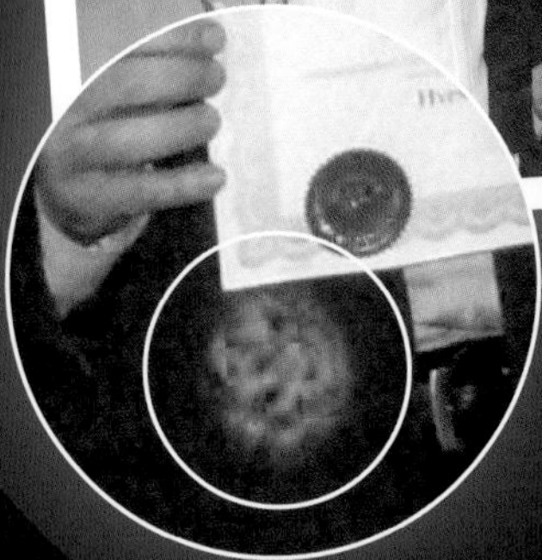

Photo 20: An orb is attached to the graduation certificate.

PREPARING FOR THE TRIATHLON

Photo 21: Preparing for the triathlon. The orbs mark places of particular health-related concerns.

ORBS AT THE DRUID CEREMONY SITE

Photo 22: An orb "observes" the equipment of a professional photographer waiting for just the right moment to "catch" an orb on his film.

WITH GOD ALL THINGS ARE POSSIBLE

ITH GOD ALL THINGS ARE POSSIBLE

MATTHEW 19:26

Photo 23: During a spiritual gathering, an orb attaches itself near the signature writing of a church in Palo Alto, California.

Photo 24: Shortly thereafter, the orb assumes an even more strategic position: the Middle East countries on the globe on the altar.

THE PHOTO SESSION
Photo 25: The newspaper photo session: 12 of 15 photos taken show orbs.

FIREWORKS ON SAN ANTONIO DAY
Photo 26: Orbs like the fireworks on St. Antonio Day in Vieste, Italy, July 2008.

WORKING FOR THE UNITY AND WELL-BEING OF ALL

Photo 27: During our presentation at a conference on orbs.

Photo 28: Same orb conference; photo taken by a different participant.

ME TOO!
Photo 29: Presentation at a symposium on orbs in Glastonbury, U.K., 2008.

MOUNTAIN LIONS
Photo 30: Orbs as children's guardians? On a trail where mountain lions had been sighted.

DANCING GIRLS
Photo 31: Orbs do like to dance with children!

Photo 32: An orb keeps company with three-year-old Krista, staging a "costume party."

BIRTHDAY PARTY AT U-TUBE
Photo 33: Birthday party at "U-Tube."
The orb chooses a strategic position to be seen.

MIRACLE ON A TRICYCLE
Photo 34: An orb accompanies a challenged two-year-old discovering the joys of life.

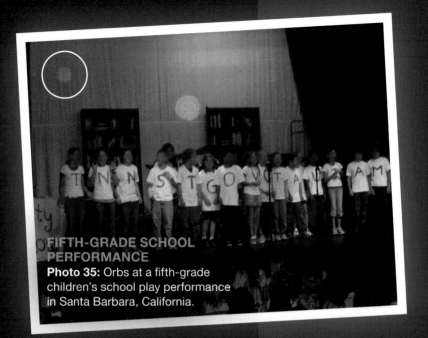

FIFTH-GRADE SCHOOL PERFORMANCE
Photo 35: Orbs at a fifth-grade children's school play performance in Santa Barbara, California.

ICE SKATING
Photo 36: Ice skating. There is approximately one orb per child in the rink.

SCIENCE AND CONSCIOUSNESS
Photo 37: Orbs at the International Conference on Science and Consciousness.

Photo 38: Orbs around a musician and his guitar.

Photo 39: J.J. and Desiree Hurtak presenting at the Science and Consciousness Conference.

Photo 40: Onye Onyemaechi (left) presenting at the 2009 Science and Consciousness Conference.

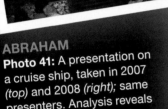

ABRAHAM
Photo 41: A presentation on a cruise ship, taken in 2007 *(top)* and 2008 *(right);* same presenters. Analysis reveals that the orbs appear to have the same interiority and may be emanations from the same Spirit Being in both cases.

DEVA PREMAL
Photo 42: Deva Premal at Grace Cathedral, San Francisco.

ELECTION OF A NEW PRESIDENT
Photo 43: Election night 2008; orb is in room, in front of TV screen—not in broadcast image.

THE HARRY RATHBUN MEMORIAL PRESENTATION
Photo 44: Harry Rathbun Memorial Lecture in the chapel of Stanford University (2007).

THE CHALICE WELL
Photo 45: High-speed orbs at Chalice Well, Glastonbury, U.K. The left one is moving upward at a velocity of approximately 5,000 mph.

Photo 46: Orbs in the church of Mount Saint Michael, featuring the poem "If."

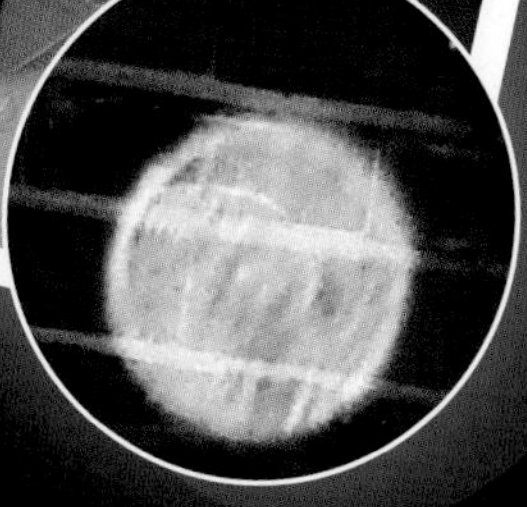

"IF"

THE PIANO
Photo 47: At our home. An orb places itself at the piano with a message.

ANGELS AND ORBS
Photo 48: Angels, orbs, and hanging ornaments.

THE RIGHT DECISION?
Photo 49: Orbs showing on request to confirm a major investment decision.

BIRTHDAY 101
Photo 50: The 101st birthday: surrounded by orbs listening in to happy memories shared.

THE PASSIONATE FLUTIST
Photo 51: The passionate flutist. Several large, bright orbs and a multitude of tiny orbs are present.

ORBS NEAR PETS
Photo 52: Dogs sensing "shaft" orbs (regular film camera recording).

THE FACES OF JANICE'S ORBS
Photo 53: Janice's orbs with faces.

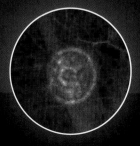

FACE IN THE SHED

Photo 54: Orbs in a deserted shed. *Top left:* original; *top right:* magnified left orb with face; *center:* enlargement of both orbs; *below:* subsequent photo with no orbs, taken to compare background features for analysis.

THE MILL ON THE FLOSS

Photo 55: An orb attaches itself to a book, triggering a profound change in the photographer's life.

Photo 56: *Left:* successive enlargements of the previous photo, revealing two faces in the orb. *Right:* same area and magnification in a subsequent photo that showed no orb at that location.

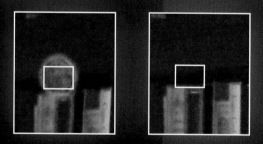

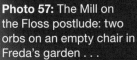

Photo 57: The Mill on the Floss postlude: two orbs on an empty chair in Freda's garden . . .

THEY ARE ALL AROUND YOU
Photo 58: Gundi surrounded by an abundant Presence from a normally hidden realm (in Abadiânia, Brazil, 2008).

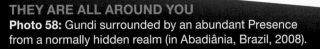

Photo 59: A chiropractor demonstrates "Network Spinal Analysis" at a spiritual retreat. An orb is "watching."

Photo 60: A healer at work. An orb is located at the far side of his head, and a second orb is near the person being healed.

Photo 61: João de Deo performs a "visible intervention" at the Casa de Dom Inácio in Abadiânia, Brazil.

Photo 62: Quantum Touch
class, visited by Spirit Beings.

Photo 63: João de Deo performs a "visible intervention";
so many beings from another dimension are present that
their visible emanations literally "cloud" the image.

THE O'JACK PHENOMENON
Photo 64: Photograph taken with a conventional point-and-shoot emulsion film camera, with the lens cap in place on the objective lens, preventing any and all light from entering the camera.

CLEAN-ROOM ORB PHOTOGRAPHY
Photo 65: Orb photograph taken in an ISO 14644-1 Class 7 clean room. Obtaining a "dust orb" under these conditions would be highly improbable.

CHAPTER ELEVEN

THEY ARE ALL AROUND YOU

*Intuition and concepts constitute the elements of all
our knowledge, so that neither concepts without an
intuition in some way corresponding to them, nor
intuition without concepts, can yield knowledge.*

— Immanuel Kant

We wrote this book to convey that there is truth and
meaning to this chapter title. The meaning lies not only
in the mere fact that Spirit Beings are around us and can
now be made visible by digital photography, such as in
Photo 58, showing Gundi in the Main Street in Abadiânia, Brazil. But more important, Spirit Beings have an
agenda for us, evidently a very positive one, which is to
"help," to assist us with every step we take.

Not every experience that falls in the category of
"orbs" can actually be documented with nice photographs of orbs. In some cases, people can actually see
them with their own eyes (or senses), as they move
around them—and in some of those cases the experience can be so strong and so profound that further

"recording," such as in photos, is entirely unnecessary. Consider the following story sent to us by Kay, a business owner in Branson West, Missouri:

> I had an experience with what may be an orb on a Wednesday evening, July 2nd, 2007. I did not know much about orbs. After learning a little about them since this experience, I thought others actually saw them as I did on this night, but now I realize most people are only seeing them on digital camera photos.
>
> That night I actually had contact with this "light energy," not only seeing it, but actually interacting with this being of intelligence. It lasted for about two hours. The "light energy" was outside my apartment in Branson, Missouri, from 10:00 P.M. until about midnight. It was originally about 30 feet above me, but came in closer to me—to only inches from my outreached hand at one point, and then at the end of these incredible two hours, it very quickly moved way up and out into the sky away from me and disappeared.
>
> It was in the form of four somewhat fuzzy white lights, rotating counter clockwise, equally spaced, around and around about four or six times. Then the four white lights (like a sheer curtain) would meet in the center, make a more solid ball of light, then sort of bounce off each other and then go back to being four separate, equally spaced faint lights, going round and round again.
>
> I had my sister in New York on the cell phone all the time while I was experiencing this unusual happening. She was scared for me and told me

to go back into the house, but I soon did not feel afraid but was rather mesmerized by the experience. When I saw it at first, it was above the roof, and I thought it was one of those advertising lights. But when I moved farther out into the parking lot, it moved with me, out above my head, and came down closer to me, always going round and round, meeting in the center, then bursting back into the four shapes of light.

I became curious, and I decided to "play" with it a little. I moved about 500 feet to a building to the left of my apartment, and it followed over me! I then decided to move up the hill to the highway, where a small strip mall is located. As I was at the crest of the hill, I reached up, still on the cell phone with my sister, and reached out my right hand. The "lights" came down very close to me. One of the four actually separated from the other three, which continued to circle in a counter clockwise fashion above and behind it, and the one light came down to almost touching my finger tips!

When this happened, I just felt this feeling of "pure love and peace"! It was wonderful! I remember just feeling totally full of love, and I remember saying to my sister on the phone, "It's beautiful! It's beautiful!" But it was not "physical" beauty, because the lights remained sort of dull, fuzzy white features (not colorful or distinctive in any way), but it was the *feeling* of "beauty" that I was experiencing. I was totally filled with the feeling of love and peace.

Then I moved up and to the right about 1,500 feet, and the lights moved above me, kept right along with me, over my head. I sat on the curb for about 20 minutes or so, talking to my sister, totally taken aback by all this. They moved up and away in the sky a bit, but still quite low above me all the while. I was watching them go round and round and meet in the center, and burst back into four separated lights.

Then I decided to go back down and around to my apartment. The light came with me. When I came down to my apartment, I actually pulled out a folding chair and placed it in the middle of the parking lot, and sat there talking to my sister—and the light was circling up above me all the time.

Then a strange thing happened. I just started to think where my camera and the new batteries were—I was thinking about taking photos of this—my friends will not believe it without "proof," and suddenly the lights moved up and way out from me, became four distinct small solid balls of light (like the pattern on a dice) and blink—lights out—and it was gone! At first, I became scared and thought, *Oh, they are going to beam me up!* But they just disappeared. I have not seen them since.

The particularly remarkable parts of this story are the duration (two hours!); the fact that a witness was connected by phone the entire time; that the beings stayed with Kay while she was walking substantial distances; the sensation of joy, peace, and love throughout the experience; and the circumstances under which the vision ended.

The duration of this extraordinary experience of about two hours is by far the longest of any such, or similar, occurrences we are aware of. It sounds like all participants, those in this world and those in the (normally) unseen realm, fully enjoyed it.

Furthermore, to our knowledge it is quite extraordinary that Kay was able to walk several thousand feet during the encounter, while the Spirit Beings stayed with her. It is reassuring that Kay felt joyful and safe during the entire duration of the encounter. Surely, these Spirit Beings were benevolent. They must have been happy that Kay recognized their presence and that she communicated it with her sister, who thus became a witness to this unfolding story.

It could well be that the Spirit Beings considered that further evidence, such as through orb photography, was superfluous, and that this is the reason why they withdrew when Kay thought of photographing them.

It is also conceivable that they disliked Kay's turning to left-brain functioning when she began to worry about being able to prove her experience to others, thus signifying that it is our right brain, the intuitive side, which orbs prefer to use for communication with humans. Since our society is primarily left-brain oriented, this would explain why the ability to see orbs and have intuitive experiences is rare for us.

Kay had a direct-intuitive encounter with benevolent beings from the other side, sensing and seeing that they were with her and surrounding her. Such direct-intuitive experiences are rare; people do not normally see or sense the presence of beings from the unseen reality surrounding them.

The photo of Gundi at the beginning of this chapter, showing her in the midst of a multitude of orbs, reminds us that this is so. They are indeed all around each of us, even though, most of the time, we are simply oblivious to this circumstance.

CHAPTER TWELVE

SPIRITUAL HEALING

Life is really about a spiritual unfolding
that is personal and enchanting—
an unfolding that no science or philosophy
or religion has yet fully clarified.

— James Redfield

Orbs have shown up in our photos during numerous alternative spiritual healing events. We have, for the longest time, wondered about what this could mean. Though there are many different types of healing modalities, it seems that the orbs don't differentiate. Could it be that they are actually there to remind us that the specific modalities aren't the important part? Are they telling us that the specific healing method is simply the particular healer's way of tapping into the realm beyond? Are they making the point that the energies used in the alternative healing arts are from their realm? Or are they possibly simply reminding us of the unity of all things? Is it possible that these Spirit Beings are present because they actually help with the healing?

MODALITIES

Network chiropractic originated about two decades ago with Donald Epstein, D.C., and is administered—quite atypical for regular chiropractic—through very gentle contacts by the practitioner with the patient's subtle energy points along the spine.

The wondrous system we call our "body" consists of trillions of components (cells) that each know how to function properly. However, the awareness of the proper context in which each of our cells has to exist may at certain occasions become compromised, and consequently, depending on the overall severity of the symptoms, we may not feel well or discover that we have contracted a disease.

In network chiropractic, these very subtle manipulations are believed to reestablish the connection to the patient's brain, the center for innate knowledge of well-being, thus reestablishing the remembrance within the cells what well-being is all about, and inducing the brain to feed back to the poorly functioning cell blocks (muscles, organs, nerves) the innate information they need for proper functioning—and thus inducing healing.

In Photo 59 we see a chiropractor demonstrating the art of network chiropractic to an audience of about 300 people at a spiritual seminar. A Spirit Being from another reality is watching.

In Photo 60 we see a famous healer tend to a patient by concentrating on her and allowing healing energy to reach her. The principle of healing used by this healer is calling on the Holy Spirit to direct Its limitless energy and power to the person in need. A spiritual healer uses no set method. Sometimes he chooses to touch the patient, at other times not; sometimes he verbalizes a message or prayer; sometimes he selects the person receiving the healing from the large audience, at other times he asks for the initiate to come forward and be healed. Note that there is also a large orb, less clearly visible, near the head of the person being healed.

In Photo 61 we present a typical orb photo taken during a "visible intervention" by healer João de Deo. Note the orb hovering above the healing scene: because the room is brightly lit and the walls are painted white, this opaque circle is almost impossible to see.

Photo 62 is a representative example of the numerous alternative healing modalities administered by practitioners all over the world. They are based on transfer of healing energy by touch to the recipient. This photo shows a class of "Quantum Touch" students.

While these photos cover a great range of healing modalities, what they have in common is that they all show orbs near the heads of the healers, the initiates, or the students. We do not think this is random; but that, instead, we deduce that there is meaning behind this positioning.

COMMONALITIES AMONG HEALING MODALITIES

If Ron can do it, you can do it!

— RON ROTH

Ron Roth, a remarkable spiritual teacher and healer, made this statement numerous times in his healing intensives. He would make his audience verbalize it over and over again—only to bring across that the art of spiritual healing is not, as is commonly believed, reserved for just a few talented individuals, but is in fact available to everybody who sets his mind to it.

We took our first Reiki Master class over ten years ago, and ever since that time, an astonishing number of notable new modalities caught our attention. The ones we have studied extensively include Network Spinal Analysis (NSA), Reiki and Karuna Reiki, Quantum Touch, Healing Touch, Jin Shin Jyutsu, Pranic Healing, Yuen Method, Matrix Energetics, and Hellinger Constellations. And this list keeps getting longer and longer.

The amazing growth of the number of healing modalities available is indeed a remarkable, hopeful indication that the idea is taking hold that there is more to healing physical illnesses than having your doctor prescribe pills.

The modalities each have their own focus, with techniques ranging from correctly placing fingers and/or hands on the recipient to using the correct breathing techniques, to the application of symbols, to intonation, to the correct imagining of colors by the practitioner.

All these techniques have their rightful place. The originators and teachers usually emphasize the simplicity of their method and that the healer's attitude is of overriding importance. His or her state of being and awareness that they are just an instrument for the divine healing energy (*prana*) to flow through to the patient are keys for the healing.

If our reading is correct that simplicity, openness, and non-attachment to the outcome are important in spiritual healing, then these attributes should be unifying factors for all the seemingly divergent, individualistic healing modalities. Then we would all recognize that each has equal significance. The one who has an inclination for chanting will use chanting in his healing sessions, a healing practitioner who is in tune with the deeper meaning of colors will do healing with colors, and a person with the gift of intuition who feels the subtle energy with her hands will position her hands on those parts of the recipient's body or aura where she feels an energetic need.

But, most important, each healer will realize that he or she is tapping into the same field of healing energy that is beyond our physical reality, the same *prana*, the same life force energy, the same repertoire of subtle energy that stimulates the innate healing capacity in the patient, not because of the healer's superior method, but—in many situations—*in spite of* the practitioner's third-dimensional[1] emphasis on a method.

Unfortunately, however, the administrators of numerous modalities have adopted one common method of teaching and practicing their art that appears contradictory to the tenets of simplicity and clean intentionality: they require several levels of study, usually taking years, before "certification" is granted. They typically make no distinction between "natural" healers who are able to quickly download the necessary information and skills with a minimum of training and others who diligently mark off all the requirements without necessarily mastering the art. They don't emphasize that it is not the diploma that qualifies a person to be a healer. There are other, overriding factors, such as humility, love, and willingness to serve.

Is the simple principle of "love," which should permeate all alternative healing modalities, at risk of being replaced with mundane "third-dimensional" requirements? Perhaps it would be desirable to replace unnecessary prerequisites for certification with more emphasis on what is really needed for this service. Should we not just get out of the way and be detached from outcome? Should we not approach every healing modality with an attitude of openness and simple service to the energies from a larger field?

We do realize that the originators of new healing modalities are, or were, highly conscious persons who neither intended nor foresaw that the modality they were teaching was anything other than an effective way of serving our fellow human beings. Not different from the emergence and subsequent evolution of new religious groupings, which unquestionably started with the purest of intentions on the part of their originators, it is probably in the second and subsequent generations where problems emerge, where ideals become rules, where methods that were reported by their originator as working well tend to become rigid requirements.

Following the trend of the times, if one teaches something that is to be received as "meaningful" in today's system of course and degree offerings, it cannot be *simple*. There has to be a complex, intellectual challenge. There cannot possibly be just one level. The entire teaching must not possibly be conveyed in one weekend. There have to be multiple levels of classes, and teaching all of them has to take up more time.

It seems that this prolific diversion into "required levels" for certification bears the risk of having one undesirable side effect that is consistently present in virtually all modalities we have experienced: it renders the pursuit of certification expensive—and out of financial reach for many potential practitioners. We hope and trust that the principle of love, which is and remains the overriding condition in all alternative healing arts modalities, outweighs all the financial limitations the aspirants of certification might have.

So what are the orbs we see in photos around healers telling us? The universe must be highly amused when looking at us. However, they know that we like to be sophisticated and love innovation, and with great patience and understanding they continuously inspire certain people with what we would call new modalities for healing. And so we have a huge variety to select from. But aren't they telling us that the commonality among all these expressions is focused attention and intention to be an instrument in the service for the highest good of the one seeking help? Couldn't it be that the Spirits from the invisible realm respond lovingly to help us out, accepting our varied approaches with a great sense of humor? Many great teachers of these modalities emphasize that you must not take yourself too seriously, and practice non-attachment to outcome!

And isn't this all confirming that someone else is doing the job? Could it be that the orbs simply want to tell us that it is not us who do the healing, but that healing is a grace granted to us from higher dimensions? Are they pointing out that we are just bystanders, and that highly evolved Spirit Beings, perhaps through the orbs that are emanating from them, are facilitating the healing? Might this be what Spirit-directed healing is all about?

THE ROLE OF ORBS IN SPIRITUAL HEALING

Photo 63 was taken by a Canadian visitor to the Casa de Dom Inácio while Medium João was performing a visible surgery to the nose of a patient. The photographer made this thoughtful statement:

I am an engineer with an analytical and mathematically structured mind. However, I have sense for novelty and am a researcher and inventor. My patents include an electronic image processing device that has been marketed for 20 years. I believe that we are part of much bigger system.

I went to Abadiânia to get clarity about a serious health challenge. I had no prior experience with orbs. At the Casa de Dom Inácio I met a person who showed me orb images he had just taken. This spurred my interest in seeing them myself. But I only had a small, old camera and thought it would be too primitive for this purpose.

I witnessed several visual interventions by Medium João. The energy level was enormous. One can observe what happens from just a few feet distance. The "surgery tools" appear to be just minimally sterilized. The patients do not react as if they experience any pain. Picture taking is welcome. "Spirits are all around us," they say, and I believed that. But when I saw them in the form of orbs in my own photo, I had a profound experience.

I own a patent on a sensor that can pick up a picture of a golf ball at the exact point of impact by the club. Every golf pro talks about the angle with which the club hits the ball. But when I can actually demonstrate this to them, it makes a huge difference.

It is similar with orb photos. Orbs are "doing" something that we cannot see with other instruments. We do see them at one particular moment of their existence, "frozen" for a fraction of a moment in a four-dimensional space-time position. This image becomes an incentive for the inventive mind to discover new concepts about their function.

When I saw this particular picture on my computer, I was excited and instantly reminded of my experiments that led to the 1989 patent. Using a very special video camera, we hoped to be able to record an image frame at a speed of 1/12,000 of a second. But there were, at first, enormous difficulties in electronically differentiating the frames—did we really see them, or did we just believe in it? As we perfected the invention, it was a great pleasure for us to go from uncertainty to a clear picture, and from there to clear knowledge.

I think this is what orb photos like this one will give us: they give us evidence about the existence of spirit beings, and from there we will eventually get to knowledge regarding what this all means.

It is indeed interesting to speculate what kind of information we can obtain if we are able to "freeze" a high-speed situation in a particular moment in time and space. We know that our eyes are unable to tell apart individual process steps if they occur in intervals shorter than about 1/25 of a second. If there were something happening in our field of view with a duration of only 1/1,000 of a second, we would not see it and not ever *consciously* know about it, either. But if we take a flash photo of it—an electronic flash lasts about 1/1000 of a second—it would clearly show up in the photo (if the flash and the event were perfectly synchronized), and we could analyze and evaluate it. This is what happens with orbs. They move too fast for our lazy eyes, but the fact that they do show up abundantly in flash photos confirms that they are ubiquitously present, move around and change their size very rapidly, and may have more than just a keen interest in certain important situations: they may actually be participants in spiritual healing.

Here is then our current thinking about how the orbs can perhaps be involved in the actual spiritual healing process.[2] We use the main characteristics of orbs,[3] which we have found to be true as the result of years of studies and consideration: super-high velocity, ability to expand and contract in size extremely quickly, and a high degree of consciousness. With these as basis we formulate a hypothesis[4] of a mechanism for Spirit-directed healing which has three components:

- Through an emanation into the physical reality (an orb), an evolved Spirit Being may be able to become active within a person's body and can, by a series of contractions of the orb to a tiny, very potent high-energy-density sphere and subsequent expansion/ relaxation to a large, low-energy-density sphere, selectively correct a deficiency, such as by breaking or reestablishing chemical bonds, or even vaporizing entire cells or cell blocks when in the high-energy-density state.

- Spirit Beings possess, or could essentially instantly acquire, the intelligence and information required for applying this ability toward the task of curing physical ailments in people. This task is then understood as an extremely long string of single energetic interventions. However, since the speed with which this could then occur is essentially unlimited, even billions of such cellular, molecular, or atomic-size "healing" events could occur within a "fraction of a moment."

- Consequently, one evolved Spirit Being alone may be capable of performing many healing events on many people within a very short physical time period.

Therefore, Spirit Beings can correct physical problems in organs or tissues using orbs to produce a superfast string of expansion-contraction events. They could do this by enabling or decoupling chemical bonds, or even vaporizing molecules or entire cells, whichever the need may be, in super-fast succession of such single events and with essentially unlimited accuracy.

This explanation is very simplistic. But it may, in fact, be compelling because of its simplicity. It shows that, even though humans have limited understanding of the spiritual realm, spiritual healing is plausible. And orb photographs, such as the ones discussed in this book, may be messages—intended by benevolent beings from the other realm—to communicate that spiritual healing is indeed real.

Let us imagine a person diagnosed with a malignant tumor. According to the first part of our hypothetical healing scenario, a Spirit Being would be capable of reducing the size of its energy field to the tiny size of tissue cells and converge that contracted, highly concentrated energy field precisely onto a spot where it is needed. This could be a cancerous cell, or a cluster of cancer cells that need to be incapacitated. It could thus do precisely what would "conventionally" be achieved with radiation therapy or chemotherapy, with the added advantage of molecular-size precision.

Depending on the amount of energy focused on the cell or onto a certain molecule within it, it could break an active bond that might be the cause for its pathological behavior. Or it could reestablish a bond that might have been broken and caused erroneous cell functioning. It could repair genetic pathology, or do whatever is required to heal cells or DNA, or entirely "vaporize" pathological tissue or isolate it from doing further damage.

According to the second part of the hypothesis, the Spirit Being would be able to instantly acquire the knowledge of precisely what is wrong with the patient. It would know which cells have what kind of pathological behavior and how to take care of that problem. It would be able to do this in extremely rapid succession, cell by cell, regardless of the total number that needs to be addressed. Analysis, contraction into the precise location, expansion . . . analysis, contraction, expansion . . . one cycle after another, trillions of times if needed, all in a fraction of a second. The cancer has spread to the lymph nodes? No problem; it would instantly know that and take care of those cells as well.

Not being subject to the physical limitations of speed, the size of the cancerous tumor would really not be of primary concern. Once done with one patient, in a fraction of an instant, the healing Spirit would be able to concentrate its attention on the next person, and the next one, and the next.

The ultimate "limitation" would only be the desire, or readiness, of the patient to get that healing "work" done. Since the patient's thought processes occur in the same realm where the Spirits operate, the two can clash, when the patient consciously or even unconsciously communicates disbelief in the ability of the Spirits to do such healings. This might then explain why so many spiritual healings do not end up with a lasting cure of the physical ailment.

The evidence at hand about orbs does indeed point to this being a possible mechanism for spiritual healing. It appears, for example, that what is happening at the Casa de Dom Inácio in Abadiânia, Brazil, supports such a scenario.

Let us first look at the invisible interventions being performed there. They are administered "simultaneously" to an entire group of as many as 100 individuals. After a short introduction and a prayer, the intervention takes place while the recipients remain seated, typically with their eyes closed and in meditative expectation. Some people can sense that something is happening to their bodies, others feel little or nothing. Nobody really knows where in the body the "surgery" is taking place. After a few minutes, the end of the session is announced, and people are ushered outside into a "recovery area." Here they are reminded that they just underwent "surgery," regardless of what they may have sensed, and need a rest period. Most people, even those who felt nothing during their intervention, will soon experience that something indeed has happened inside their bodies and will gladly follow the suggested resting instructions.

Our hypothesis agrees with the sequence of events. The pre-selection process meets the requirement that the patient must be the initiator for the process to be successful. The group situation and the short time required for the interventions of all people in the group are plausible due to the high velocities available in the spiritual reality. The finding that many patients do not even sense that a surgery has taken place follows from the circumstance that no incision is required for the surgery; only a minimum number of nerve cells, if any, are affected and the surgery does not damage unnecessary amounts of healthy tissue but is confined to the pathological cells, organs, or tissue.

The need for the patient to take time to recuperate is understandable—after all, an intervention on the physical body has taken place, and weakness and soreness afterward should be expected. It is said that certain people who worked in the medical field during their lifetimes are now the Spirit Beings performing many of the surgeries at the Casa. The fact that many Spirit Entities do not have that "background" and nevertheless are as effective as those who do, confirms that the actual knowledge required to perform these surgical interventions can be acquired by any evolved Spirit Being. It may, however, be true that in the spirit world, just as much as in our physical world, Spirit Beings do what they like to do and are inclined to do. This may explain why those who had medical "careers" in their human lifetimes may more likely want to lend their talents to the cause of spiritual healing than others who followed different pursuits in their lifetime.

Let us now look at *visible* surgical interventions performed at the Casa de Dom Inácio, or at the kind of healing practiced by renowned spiritual healers as it relates to our hypothesis about spiritual, or invisible, healing. It turns out that visible interventions may not be so different from invisible interventions as it appears at first glance. The energy "zapping" that many people experience when touched by a healer like Ron Roth or Richard Bartlett may be the healing action performed by a Spirit Being in accordance with our hypothesis. The sensation experienced by people in such circumstances—swaying, soft knees, a certain weakness during hours or even days following such an event, and the miraculous healings reported at large—do fit the pattern described here.

The phenomenon of visible spiritual surgical interventions at the Casa de Dom Inácio and at various other locations, mostly in Brazil and the Philippines, is extremely interesting. For example, the people connected to the Casa insist that, as far as healing is concerned, invisible and visible surgeries are equally effective. They state that the primary reason for visible surgeries is for the benefit of the onlookers, or even the patient himself.[5] They will be more easily convinced of the healing power of the Spirit Beings when they see an actual surgery and witness how it happens: no anesthesia, almost no pain when excruciating suffering would otherwise be the norm, almost no bleeding, and essentially no scars remaining from the incision.

Our hypothetical scenario may very well explain this if one looks at surgery as a two-stage process: first, the actual visible procedure (incision, the scraping of the eye with a simple knife, or the insertion of a long metal tool up though the nostrils) and second, the actual "work" on the pathological tissue.

The first stage would be an enormous effort—again via directed contraction and expansion sequences of the energy field of Spirit emanations—for no other reason than to demonstrate that it is possible for Spirit Beings to do all this. Taking care of the incision, no bleeding, no pain, no need for anesthesia, all this would happen in accordance with the hypothesis: an almost endless string of molecular-level events involving a super-fast chain of Spirit-guided contractions and expansions of energetic Spirit-emanated spheres. All this would be done to "disguise" and/or "deactivate" the physical impact on the patient of the crude incisions done by the healer in this "visible" part of the surgery.

The second stage would be the actual act of healing, as described above for invisible interventions. This second stage would really not be in any substantive way connected with the first stage. The first stage would be mostly to satisfy human curiosity; the second would be the true act of healing from whatever ailment afflicts the patient.

CHAPTER THIRTEEN

THE O'JACK PHENOMENON

For those who believe, no words are necessary. For those who do not believe, no words are possible.

— Saint Ignatius of Loyola

We conclude the book with a chapter on a phenomenon that has many aspects in common with orbs but is, in other aspects, even more perplexing and more revealing, and gives further clues on the mechanism of orb photography.

The foreword by Dr. William Tiller to *The Orb Project* included two photographs. They were so unusual that at first glance, Klaus hesitated to include them in the book. They showed a photograph with the camera's lens cap covering the lens.

Soon after the book was published, Klaus was contacted by a person named Dr. Stanislav O'Jack, who introduced himself as the photographer who had taken those photos. Their first call lasted at least an hour, and both felt that a kinship had developed between them that must have started much, much earlier—except they could not pinpoint its origin. Many more phone conversations ensued, followed by a weekend get-together by the ocean, together with spouses. Orbs, alternative healing, and of course anomalous photography were the topics explored.

Stanislav asked Klaus to buy a roll of film and insert it into his slightly antiquated emulsion film point-and-shoot camera. After Klaus had carefully inspected it and found it perfectly normal, he put the lens cap back on the camera, and the four of us went off to a photo shooting session at the famous "Sea Ranch Chapel."

Dr. O'Jack would conscientiously take note of each photo taken, clearly describing the scene ("target"), position of the lens cap ("on" or "off"), date and time, and various other details. We actually took some pictures of him photographing. All of the 24 exposures were taken with the lens cap in place—and about two-thirds of these resulted in fully exposed color photos, such as Photo 64, showing Stanislav's wife Helen (left) and Gundi in front of The Sea Ranch Chapel.

What does photography with the lens cap in place have to do with orbs? Why would we include such an experiment in this book? The answer will unfold. It has to do with the focus and intent of the photographer. But let's develop the story in proper sequence.

We first deal with the obvious question, "Where is the trick or fraud?" The answer is simple, yet for many readers—and we cannot blame any of them for it—entirely unacceptable: there is none. There is no fraud; there is no trick. We personally examined the camera with due diligence, but, more important, Dr. O'Jack's integrity and honesty are beyond reproach. It is simply unthinkable that these pictures are anything but real.

In Appendix C we present a closer analysis of Dr. O'Jack's photos and come up with a preliminary explanation. Obviously, it cannot be regular natural light as we know it that produces the lens-capped photos. It could not pass through the lens cap. But if some other variation of light were present that has the same wavelength spectrum of natural light but has only about 1/10 of its frequency, such a form of light, or radiation, could indeed penetrate through the lens cap, be diffracted just the same in the camera lens, and produce Dr. O'Jack's phenomenal photos.

The notion that lower frequencies produce the phenomenal effect is contrary to the common perception among people interested in spirituality. They typically think that the spiritual, the "higher," the "better" should have higher, not lower frequencies or "vibrations." The O'Jack photos indicate that it might at times be more appropriate to talk in terms of "different," rather than "raised" frequencies as the desirable state of being or course of action. (See also Endnote 1, in which we make a case for talking about "raised amplitudes" instead of "raised vibrations.")

Perhaps the most significant conclusion from the O'Jack Phenomenon is that it is intimately involved ("entangled") with the photographer himself. We personally have not been able to reproduce Dr. O'Jack's results, nor do we know many other people who have demonstrated similar photos;[2] nor has Dr. O'Jack been able to predict success in every attempt. A good fraction of his lens-capped photo attempts predictably yield black photos.

So what is different about Dr. O'Jack? First of all, he is too modest a man to claim anything that is special about him compared to others. What we do know, though, is that for decades Dr. O'Jack has rigorously practiced daily meditation. Might his spiritual maturity be the deciding difference?

There would certainly seem to be validity to this train of thought, when one takes into consideration Dr. William Tiller's famous psychoenergetic experiments with intention-imprinted devices. Without doubt, prolonged intense meditative focusing of specific intention onto the subject of his experiments, such as raising or lowering the pH value of water, would be the prerequisite for realizing the intended effect.[3]

Clearly the last word has not been spoken with regard to Dr. O'Jack's through-the-lens-cap photography and Dr. Tiller's focused-intention experiments. But what they do indicate—and this they do beyond doubt—is that the power of focused attention is very real and can manifest in effects that can be measured with regular scientific equipment, such as a photo camera in the case of Dr. O'Jack, and simple, standard electronic measuring devices in the case of Professor Tiller's work.

The biggest unanswered question then remains how the intention of the photographer can possibly manifest such that sufficient energy is generated to reflect off *all* the objects imaged in the photo and cause the photographic imprint in the camera. Might the energy of the camera flash be utilized in this process in a way that the photographer's mind functions more as a catalyst than as an energy source?

If this were the case, we could more easily rationalize the situation from an energetic consideration; yet a fundamental question would remain how subtle energy originating in the mind of a person could convert a substantial fraction of the photon energy from a photo camera flash into a physically unknown form of light of lesser energy content and a wavelength spectrum similar to that of regular light.

It is thinkable that what we know about orb photography falls along the same line of reasoning. For example, it has been reported by numerous orb photographers that, once they set their mind to seeing orbs in their photos, their yield of orbs in the photos—though not predictable in every instance—will be considerably higher than the yield obtained by a person who is not in tune with such energies, such as a skeptic would be. We have ourselves seen an increase of our yield of orbs in our photos by a factor of approximately 100, and similar orb yield increases have been reported by other orb photographers.

This could mean there is an interaction of the conscious Spirit Being emanating an orb with the subtle focused thought or intention energy emanating from the orb photographer. It would utilize the energy from the flash incident upon the orb and convert that energy into a highly directed beam of radiation of wavelengths in the visible light spectrum and lower frequencies than those of regular light. The lower frequencies would permit the radiation from the orb to reach the camera through a wide-open lens, not impeded by the iris which is, in most cases, made of plastic material that is opaque to regular visible light but translucent to radiation at lower frequencies.

Looking at the overall energetics of this process, it becomes apparent that orb photography would be much "easier" than through-the-lens-cap photography. As we stated elsewhere in this book, it takes only a few hundred highly directed photons to produce an orb image, which is certainly several orders of magnitude fewer photons than are required to produce the entire lens-capped photo. Furthermore, the consciousness of the Spirit Being itself (from which the "orb" is an emanation) could conceivably play a role in catalyzing the energy conversion. The photographer would thus "only" have to function as a "communicator" with the Spirit Being. He would, perhaps, be the motivator for the orb to catalyze the conversion of energy from the flash into lower frequency radiation that is then directed by the Spirit Entity into the photographer's camera.

CHAPTER FOURTEEN

EXPANDED PERSPECTIVE

The longest journey is the journey inwards.

— Dag Hammarskjöld

It is our personal interpretation that the orb phenomena, as well as many other supernatural phenomena mankind has witnessed over the ages, have been given to us collectively from the unseen reality as pointers. They cast light on an issue, point the way to a solution of a specific problem, encourage, give an "aha" experience. If we are so inclined, we are invited to personalize what we see.

This is not an exact science. Nothing that has to do with consciousness is an exact science. There is no guarantee for reproducibility. What applies to one does not necessarily apply to another person, and vice versa.

The world of consciousness, from which the orbs are messengers, is a realm in which other laws apply than those that pertain to the physical reality. The laws are not absolute but relative. The confinement to space and time, as we know it, does not exist. Speeds of processes, even though likely still sequential, can be much, much faster than in the physical realm.

Klaus was brought up with the notion that what we can see, hear, smell, touch, feel, and yes, calculate and rationalize is all there is. From his early childhood he remembers being taught that there are "real" aspects to life, and then there are fairy tales; only the "real" experiences in life ultimately matter. He was also told to believe in a life after death. But then, whenever he asked a pointed question about how that life would be, to better understand, he was be repudiated for having the audacity of asking such "inappropriate" questions. He was told, "These are things, spiritual matters you have to *believe* in, but these things are not to be taken for 'real,' because, after all, there are no angels in the real world, and death is the end of all life, and every well-educated person knows that."

What were the teachings in your formative years? Did you have an experience seeing a deceased loved one's spirit appear to you, or did you see a person next to your mother, and did she not see it and told you, "I love you, but there is nobody"? Or did you ever hear a voice your father did not hear, and he labeled you a dreamer? Did the correct answer to a math question in a test just pop into your mind, and the teacher would take you to the principal, because you obviously cheated?

It is important to honor what we were given in our early years, and how we learned about reality. Everyone who grew up with experiences like this would have quickly learned to stop asking questions about such "strange" things. We all want to be normal, and a normal person does not believe in imaginative things. As we grow older and acquire more education, this differentiation between the "acceptable" view of reality and the "unacceptable" intuitive part of ourselves becomes more and more rigid. The teachings in our basic physics and engineering classes would further fortify this view; there simply is nothing that is beyond the speed of light, nothing that is lighter and faster than a photon, we were told, and our mind is a not yet entirely understood agglomeration of physical matter undergoing physiochemical reactions.

It is our hope that this book entices you to reconsider such conditioning. No longer, so we hope, can one state that there are no angels, merely because we cannot see them. No longer can one deny that life after life exists, merely because we cannot see what we can accept as credible evidence of it. No longer can we say that there is no such thing as a valid "hunch," because we must, of course, be able to do everything we undertake on calculable rationale.

Though there was nothing to authenticate such things in the past, now the orbs show us something different. Granted, they do not bluntly paint the picture of people with wings; it's a bit more complicated than that. They do not simply tell us that we will be living another thousand years after we die, and we will then see those who are still living in this reality, but they will not be able to see us! Nor do they tell us that we should stop going to school and, from here on, only act upon what we "feel" in the moment. They are inviting us to expand our perception to a larger context.

It continues to be our rationale that the orbs are emanations from Spirit Beings. This means in a nutshell that our reality does not end at the end of our current perception of physics; i.e., the speed of light or the most modern particle physics. It extends, instead, far, far beyond that, by many orders of magnitude, into a realm that, just as ours, encompasses sentient beings— probably more intelligent beings than we find in our physical reality.

This reality, we are beginning to find out, is also fundamentally based on "energy," just as ours is. However, in terms of the quantity and character of the physical energy that we have come to know about in our reality, the energy in the realm beyond ours is "small," refined, "subtle." For that energy to do something in our physical reality, it would be like you or us trying to force a freight train back into motion by sheer muscle power when it has stopped in its tracks. It's possible, but highly improbable, unless . . .

So, what is it that we would have to do if we wanted to demonstrate to someone that we can, in fact, get that train rolling again? We would have to be smart. For a long time, for almost as long as life on Earth has existed, we would not have been able to do anything like that, because our muscle power would simply not have been sufficient. But then, in the latest speck of time (compared to the four billion years that our Earth has existed), we learned to devise machines that generate power. We were smart, and with our smartness we would eventually come up with the means to get the train rolling.

And so it is with the world of spirits when it comes to proving their existence to us. Spirit Beings are smart, probably very smart, but it is still utterly difficult for them to demonstrate to us that they exist, because we have been so locked into the freight train mentality (thinking that our muscles are not sufficient to move it), and we have not looked at other possibilities . . . yet.

With the discovery of orbs, this has changed. With our invention of digital photography, we ourselves, not the Spirits, have created a simple—or perhaps not really all that simple, but an extremely widespread and literally ubiquitously available—method to see something with our bare eyes which was generated at the expense of an extremely tiny quantity of physical energy.

Similarly small amounts of energy are used inside of many electronic devices, but the devices will only work if huge numbers of such minute-energy steps are strung together in the correct sequence. When it comes to digital photography, this is fundamentally different. Here just a few photons—the smallest of small amounts of physical energy—are required to generate something that you and I can hold in our hand and see, look at for hours, and pass on to others. We can print them as images on paper, or post them on the Internet for thousands to view whenever they want to. We have, finally, invented the locomotive that Spirit Beings can use to make themselves known.

To generate such minute amounts of energy as are required for recording orb-like features in digital photographs is within their reach. Even then, it appears that they can generate these minute energies not from their own energy reservoir in their own realm, but by simply converting them from physical energy that we nonchalantly offer to them when we take our digital photographs, i.e., from the electronic flash.

Digital photography is perhaps two decades old. And it came along with an electronic flash that can generate "real" physical images of real objects, such as airborne particles that can be explained simply on the basis of reflection of the photons from the flash at them. While this process is very different from that of "producing" genuine orbs, the end product often looks quite similar.

Unfortunately, even though the vast majority of orbs observed by people all over the world are real, this has no bearing on skeptics who continue with their argument—that because flash reflections at airborne particles resemble orbs, all such images must therefore be reflections at airborne particulates. It is of little avail to try to convince such critics otherwise, just as it was of little avail to convince the clerical echelons in the 16th century that the earth was revolving around the sun.

Nevertheless, we can attempt to advance the credibility of orb photography through the power of statistics, which is a power most critics actually *do* believe in. We have demonstrated that in many orb photographs a meaning can be derived from either the positioning of the orbs in the photo or their interior appearance. We have given numerous examples where the positioning or interiority of orbs is unique and not just statistically random. This does imply that, on the basis of statistics, there is more relevance to orb photos than to pictures of reflections at airborne particles, which would, without further argument, follow the laws of random statistical distribution.

We must, in this context, then also understand that, at present, this is all these Spirit Beings can demonstrate to us through orb photos. They can appear visually, but they cannot talk, and they cannot write.[1] They cannot give us messages in the way we are used to getting them.

It is quite possible that this is, in fact, so by immensely wise divine design. For what real possibility of evolving into a consciousness-producing species would humankind have, if it knew, *beyond a shadow of a doubt,* what the good course of action might be? Of course, everybody would then choose the good, and there would then not be a *real* basis for a choice and thus no real possibility to advance in consciousness. For is it not ultimately that by *not* knowing everything we have the possibility to grow in consciousness? It seems that the most ingenious "invention" ever conceived was that of the free will of the human being, who would, by virtue of *being required to* discern between good and evil, become capable of "producing" consciousness and, thus, evolve his soul and, ultimately, his own creator: conscious consciousness evolving itself, by design, to higher and higher echelons![2]

This is then why we must do our part to decipher messages from Spirit Beings through orbs. It is not mechanical. It requires of us, first and foremost, opening ourselves to the possibility that our orb photos contain messages. We must then perfect the art of perceiving them. With the examples we have given in this book, we hope you may be able to expand your innate capacity to perceive and read such messages.

Messengers from the other realm are assisting us on our journey toward wholeness and seem to reach us in ever-changing forms. It is easy to conclude that there is a mighty force out there, willing to help us expand our perception, so we become more responsive, loving human beings. Could it be that, as we tune in to the signals they give us, our innate creative potential will unfold and lead us to new discoveries that will benefit us all?

CHAPTER FIFTEEN

WHERE DO WE GO FROM HERE?

*The true nature of anything
is the highest it can become.*

— Aristotle

In the previous pages we enthusiastically shared a few examples of orbs and their stories as people experienced them. We hope this will inspire your own exploration and search for meaning connected to these phenomena.

Throughout the ages, mankind has received messages and helpful hints through symbols and signs appearing in various forms.

This seems to tell us that we are not alone but are assisted and guided to realize increased quality of life for all. We now know that there is a field of knowledge, wisdom, intelligence, a field of infinite possibilities to tap into. Transmissions from this field, which some call

"Morphic Field," occurs in various forms and numerous creative ways. Patiently, with great ingenuity, diverse signals are broadcast toward us to induce us to pay attention. Perhaps it is time to listen with our heart and playfully test the hunches we are receiving from this vast, invisible resource. We may discover how help from out there reaches us in the here and now.

Tune into the limitless field of possibilities to receive answers to your questions! There are great opportunities waiting for us, as we allow our innocent, curious sense of discovery guide us to more.

CLEAN-ROOM ORB PHOTOGRAPHY

Photo 65 was taken in January 2009, by Drs. Andreas Burkart and Ulrich Volz (Konstanz, Germany) under ISO 14644-1 Class 7 clean-room conditions. The photo is essential proof that the orb cannot be explained as due to reflection at an airborne particle.

These clean-room conditions specify that the probability of an airborne particle of 5 micrometer size within the "orb zone" of a digital camera (approximately within 1 cubic inch in front of the lens) is about 1 in 20. Larger particles are not permitted. This must be compared with the simple geometric requirement that a hypothetical dust particle that caused the orb in Photo 65 would have had to be approximately 500 micrometers in size, i.e., 100 times larger than the largest particles permitted under these clean-room conditions. Given these numbers, we can safely state that the orb observed in this photo—albeit showing up at low contrast—is not due to a reflection off an airborne particle.

The authors of this photo state:

Inspired by the scientific approach taken in *The Orb Project,* we got the idea of conducting an experiment in a medical clean room which we use for dental research and development projects. Evidence of orbs taken in a "clean room" that is free of dust and water particles clearly establishes that the concept of explaining orbs on the basis of such particles must be excluded and indicates presence of an energetic phenomenon. In this photo we can unquestionably, albeit at low contrast, discern an orb in the vicinity of other people. A report issued by the medical products firm KLS Martin Group confirms the clean room criteria.

ON THE AUTHENTICITY OF ORBS

The most prevalent argument against the authenticity of orbs is that they are believed to be reflections off airborne particles positioned in close vicinity to the camera's objective lens. While it is true that flash reflections reflected off small dust particles and droplets suspended within a few centimeters in front of the camera lens (the "orb zone"), can indeed cause orb-like image features, this explanation cannot be upheld for the immense quantities of orb photographs taken by thousands of people all over the world. Common counterarguments against the airborne particle reflection theory (the orb zone theory) are summarized as follows:

- *Distance:* Many orb photographers have taken and reported photographs in which an orb is "eclipsed" by an object that is located several feet away from the camera. These could not be airborne particles, then, because they are far outside the orb zone.

- *Numbers:* Dr. Míceál Ledwith, co-author of *The Orb Project,* has taken well over 300,000

orb photos. We ourselves have thousands
in electronic storage, and we know others
who have similar archives of orb photos.
It is unreasonable to categorically state
that all of these photos must—on grounds
that there is no "satisfactory" scientific
explanation—be artificial.

- *Clarity:* If objects are located very close to
  the camera, such as they have to be for
  the "orb zone" theory to work, they will
  appear fuzzy and ill-defined. This is due
  to depth-of-field limitations of the camera
  lens. If objects are just a few centimeters
  from the camera, they appear completely
  out of focus. Yet orbs appear with the same
  brilliance and sharpness no matter how
  close or far away they are from the camera.

- *Photo to photo changes:* When several
  photographs are taken in rapid succession,
  one would expect roughly the same number
  of orb-like reflections in each photo if they
  were airborne particles—perhaps not at
  the same locations, but roughly the same
  number. Instead, many orb photographers
  have noted that they often see a photo
  exhibiting one or a multitude of orbs,
  followed with several photos showing no
  orbs, then another one with many orbs, and
  so on. It is unrealistic to assume that the
  distribution of airborne particulates is so
  irregular that multitudes of them are near

the camera at one particular time, then gone a few seconds earlier or later.

- *Static locations:* Airborne particles are constantly moving, so it would be all but impossible to expect the same airborne particle to be in essentially the same location in two photos taken several seconds apart. However, we have repeatedly observed what appears to be the same orb in consecutive photos.

- *High speeds:* Many images of orbs show them in fast motion, with velocities calculated at over 500 miles per hour, and at possibly even much higher speeds. But airborne particles do not move that fast. There have been numerous reports, including in *The Orb Project,* of experiments with deliberately produced reflection images of airborne dust particles or water droplets. They cannot attain such high velocities as are often seen in genuine orb images.

- *Asymmetric internal features:* Genuine orbs often exhibit very distinct internal features, including voids, which would be very hard to explain if the image came from a reflection off tiny airborne particles, droplets, insects, or the like. At times, the internal appearance in orbs can be strikingly similar to human faces.

- *Clean room orbs:* Clean rooms are used in research laboratories where it is vitally important to guarantee that no airborne particles above a certain size are present in the air that could deposit on the research specimens, such as a wafer in semiconductor device fabrication. We have recently obtained evidence that it is possible to photograph orbs under ISO 14644-1 Class 7 clean room conditions.[1]

Other arguments brought forth by some critics center around impurities or abnormalities related to the camera and the electronic recording device built into the camera. This class of arguments can be dismissed with any of the following observations:

- *Successive photos of different scenes:* camera defects can be identified easily and without ambiguity. They would have to be expected to repeat themselves in successive photos, regardless of the scene photographed. Serious orb photographers routinely check their photos and cameras against this sort of defect and will never identify an orb as genuine, if a camera defect cannot be excluded.

- *Film type irrelevant:* While the overwhelming majority of orb photographers use digital cameras, photographers using point-and-shoot film cameras often take good orb images too. Dutch professional photographer Ed Vos has taken and published numerous photos of orbs on conventional film (see Chapter 1, endnote 2).

* *CCD vs. CMOS:* The vast majority of digital cameras are based on CCD (charge-coupled device) recording devices. However, there is another, entirely different image sensor technology, CMOS (complementary metal oxide semiconductor), which is used in a few higher-end digital camera models (see Introduction endnote 3 for details). CMOS cameras have a much smaller effective sensor surface to record plate surface compared to CCD cameras. Therefore, CMOS cameras require much more light intensity to record orbs. Our experiments with a new Nikon D5000 CMOS camera confirm that the number of orbs obtained with that camera is notably lower than what we are typically getting with our CCD cameras, and the interior resolution of the orbs is inferior. In terms of sensitivity and image buildup mechanism, a CMOS camera is probably more comparable to a conventional film camera than a CCD device.

ON THE O'JACK PHENOMENON

Building on the first few pages of Chapter 13, we want to examine the O'Jack Phenomenon a bit more in depth. Let's take a closer look at the pictures Dr. O'Jack took that afternoon near the Sea Ranch Chapel in Northern California.

- Dr. O'Jack's images look like normal photos taken under normal imaging conditions, with the lens cap off. There is no evidence of image distortion. Nothing is missing in the image. The features in the foreground are as perfectly imaged as those in the background.

- The photo is in focus, everywhere across the imaged field; there is nothing washed out anywhere in any of the lens-capped photos; no evidence of astigmatism or unidirectional blurring, such as might occur due to motion during the exposure.

- The colors in the lens-capped photos are pristine, uniform across the image, and in

all apparent ways the same as in normal
color photos. (The image shown in Photo
64 was rather crudely scanned from the
original color photo print, and the colors
were muted in that scanning process.)

In short, the lens-capped photos are in all obvious
photographic details identical to those that a normal
photographer would expect when taken with a normal,
state-of-the-art digital or conventional film still-photo
camera, albeit with the lens cap removed.

At this point, it should also be mentioned that Dr.
O'Jack has taken such photos, with the lens cap in place,
around the world, on and off for three decades. He has
used different brands (Kodak, Canon, Nikon), and occasionally takes lens-capped photos with a digital camera,
too (Nikon Coolpix with 10 megapixels). The cameras
usually have automatic flash, but occasionally he has
gotten a photo without the flash. He prefers low-speed
(low ASA) film (however, Photo 64 was taken with regular 100 ASA film) because it seems to him that a lower
speed film produces nicer photos. The photos are usually
taken with 1/25-second shutter speed and a wide open
aperture (since the automatic camera had obviously assumed darkness behind the capped lens).

To try to explain such a phenomenon from a rational engineering/technical/physics frame of mind
is doomed to fail, and no matter how complicated or
simple our attempt at an explanation, a critical reader
would be able to shoot it down as "nonsense." But then,
as we discussed earlier, when we come to the fringes of
the physical reality, such as we are dealing with here,
"sense" and "nonsense" have to be redefined.

Let us now, with this caveat in mind, look at how these astonishing photos can possibly come about. Dr. O'Jack's impeccable integrity makes the task of looking at this phenomenon somewhat easier, as we do not have to assume foul play with regard to any of the above-listed experimental data. We do not have to deal with argumentation like "this cannot be"—"cannot be" does not apply, because *it is*. So we can delve right into attempts for an explanation.

An analysis, which is undoubtedly superficial yet intriguing in its simplicity, suggests the following hypothesis:

If there were a form of electromagnetic radiation having the same wavelength spectrum as regular visible light but a frequency of only about 1/10 of that of regular light (which means an energy equivalent of about 0.25 electron volts; propagating at 1/10 of the speed of light), this could in principle explain the technical aspect of Dr. O'Jack's lens cap photography.

Our hypothesis is based on the assumption that Dr. O'Jack's through-the-lens-cap ("TTLC") photos come about via the normal photographic process. All indications point in that direction. The same field of view was imaged that would be expected for a normal photograph; the image is in focus throughout; the colors are correctly presented—in short there is no image detail that suggests that the radiation that produced the TTLC image is of a nature other than normal electromagnetic radiation with a wavelength spectrum of that of regular visible light, i.e., ranging from approximately 0.4 to 0.8 micrometers. Clearly, regular light cannot penetrate the lens cap; so another mechanism or another type of radiation has to be assumed.

The big leap in thought would then be to entertain the idea that there might be some other electromagnetic radiation that comes into play here. Since the wavelength spectrum is supposed to be unchanged, it must be the frequency that is different from regular light. In regular light, the product of wavelength and frequency equals the speed of light. If we hold the wavelength constant and vary the frequency, this new radiation will then be faster or slower than the speed of light, depending on the frequency being higher or lower than that of regular light.

Typically, radiation of higher frequencies than those of visible light would not be able to penetrate as easily through plastic materials or even glass as visible light does, and we have to rule out higher frequencies on this count alone.

On the other hand, the transmissivity of plastic materials and glass generally improves with decreasing frequency of the incident radiation. So going to lower frequencies overcomes one of the hurdles: it could explain why the radiation that caused Dr. O'Jack's TTLC photos penetrates through the plastic lens cap.

But there are other factors to consider. Whatever radiation we are dealing with must be sufficiently energetic to dissociate the silver halide molecules in the photographic film. The dissociation energy of silver chloride (AgCl) is approximately 1/4 of an electron volt (eV). We must conclude that the radiation we are dealing with in photos has an energy higher than that. The photon energy of visible light is about 2.5eV, or about 10 times the AgCl dissociation energy. This would limit the frequency of the radiation we are trying to define to about 1/10 of the frequency of regular light. It turns out that infrared radiation of that frequency does indeed penetrate plastic materials of the type used in lens caps reasonably well.

This renders radiation of the type defined in our hypothesis as a feasible candidate for TTLC photography, the wavelength spectrum being the same as that of visible light, and the frequency being that of near-infrared light, about a factor 10 lower than that of visible light.

Dr. O'Jack's experimental data appear to be congruent with these assumptions, including his observation that low-speed film emulsions work "significantly better" than high-speed films. Lower speed emulsions require more AgCl molecules to be dissociated per image element than high-speed emulsions. Low-speed emulsions are, therefore thicker than high-speed emulsions. Since our low-frequency radiation tends to be less easily absorbed by amorphous materials, including photo emulsions, than higher frequency radiation, it would indeed be advantageous to record the TTLC images on thicker, i.e., lower-speed, emulsions.

A specific series of further experiments could easily confirm or disprove our hypothesis. If Dr. O'Jack were inclined to undertake more experiments with TTLC photography, it would be interesting to examine what happens if he affixes some material to the lens cap that is impervious to near-infrared radiation, such as aluminum foil. Our hypothesis would be disproved if he would still be able to record TTLC photos with such a lens cap.

This hypothesis is, of course, very pragmatic and excludes any esoteric explanations. The marvels of existence, as they are unfolding in view of the latest extrapolations from quantum theory, would offer much more "elegant" explanations of this and similar phenomena, explanations that would not require any attempt at all to rationalize them based on conventional physics.

With regard to the questions that are still unanswered by our hypothetical explanation, they are substantial. Where would light propagating at 1/10 the speed of light come from? Looking at it from a conventional physics point of view, such radiation doesn't exist. There is no light known that has these characteristics. It simply cannot be! But so is a photo taken with the lens cap on the camera lens. It cannot be! It is physically impossible! Yet . . . it *is*, we have undeniable proof of it. Clearly, we have to go outside of conventional physics and consider other clues for the explanation of our phenomenon.

Photo Credits

If a credit is not given, the photo was taken by Klaus Heinemann or Gundi Heinemann.

Photo 2: Photo taken at Orbs Conference near Hude, Germany, June 2008.

Photo 4: Photo taken March 26, 2008 at 9:03 p.m., La Fonda Hotel, Santa Fe, N.M.

Photo 5: Photo courtesy of Renee Pisarz; Renee Pisarz communicated her experiences related to the death of her son in "Angel 54: A Mother's Sacred Journey from Grief to Healing," available at www.booklocker.com:80/books/3822.html.

Photo 6: Photo courtesy of Carola M.

Photo 12: Photo taken June 2008, on board of the Nordam of Holland America Line.

Photo 13: Taken about an hour later, same venue.

Photo 14: The Battistero at Pisa, Italy. Photos taken about two minutes apart. *Top:* Photo taken during the tour guide's explanation of the importance of the Saint Mary statue above the entrance. *Bottom:* Photo taken when she had switched the topic to the fact that the Baptistry is also leaning.

Photo 15: Photo taken in San Giovanni Rotondo, Italy, 2008.

Photo 16: Taken from the hotel room in Hindelang, Germany, June 2008.

Photo 17: Taken a minute later from the same location, in a different direction into the night sky, upon request of the skeptic.

Photos 18 and 19: Photos courtesy of Leslie Rhonda, 2009.

Photo 20: Photo courtesy of Robert Maday, 2008.

Photo 21: Near Hude, Germany, during an Orbs Conference, June 2008.

Photo 23: Upon close analysis of the photo, the orb is actually located above the head of the person in the foreground. However, due to the lack of 3-D definitions in the photo, the orb appears to be attached to the globe.

Photo 25: Photo courtesy of Linda Horton, taken March 22, 2008. Note that no electronic enhancement was applied.

Photo 26: Photo courtesy of Amanda Bayer, taken March 22, 2008 at the beginning of our presentation.

Photo 27: Photo courtesy of Sandra Underwood, taken July 13, 2008 at the Prophets Conference on Orbs and Phenomena in Glastonbury, U.K.

Photo 29: Photo courtesy of Lorraine, December 2008.

Photo 30: Photo courtesy of Connie Maday.

Photo 36: Dr. Rupert Sheldrake at the Tenth International Conference on Science and Consciousness, Santa Fe, N.M., April 2, 2008; the close-up photo was contrast enhanced to bring out the features of the orb at the picture of the Earth.

Photo 37: Photo taken at the Tenth International Conference on Science and Consciousness, Santa Fe, NM, April 2, 2008; the close-up photo was contrast enhanced to bring out the features of the orb below the person's hand.

Photo 39: Eleventh International Conference on Science and Consciousness, Santa Fe, N.M., March 30, 2009.

Photo 40: Left picture taken on July 8, 2007, right taken on June 1, 2008, on the same stage. Note that the right picture was taken with a telephoto lens.

Photo 41: Photo taken on September 19, 2008, at Grace Cathedral in San Francisco, Calif.

Photo 48: Image contrast was enhanced in the section enlargement to bring out the features of the ornaments.

Photo 50: Photo courtesy of Elke Paul.

Photo 51: Photo courtesy of Lisa and Amy Bradley.

Photo 52: Photo courtesy of Susan Strine and Sandra Sanders.

Photo 53: Photos and courtesy of Janice Driver, Sutton, Surrey, U.K., January 2009.

Photo 54: Taken in June 2008.

Photos 55, 56, and 57: Photos courtesy of Freda Chaney, Mount Vernon, Ohio, February—November 2009.

Photo 58: Photo taken in Abadiânia, Brazil, 2008.

Photo 62: The Quantum Touch class was taught by Gundi Heinemann (second from right, top row) in Sunnyvale, Calif., September 18, 2007.

Photo 63: Photo courtesy of Goran Spasovsky, Canada, 2009.

Endnotes

Introductory Note

1. Míceál Ledwith and Klaus Heinemann, *The Orb Project* (New York: Simon & Schuster, 2007), also available in German, Italian, Dutch, Russian, and other languages.

Introduction

1. It is important to clarify what we understand as physical, nonphysical, extraterrestrial, and spiritual. In the context of this book, *physical* means everything that is subject to time and space and follows the laws of Newtonian and mainstream quantum physics. With that definition, the fastest speed in the physical reality is the speed of light, and certain results from quantum physics that point at faster speeds would fall in the "nonphysical" realm. This definition is a concession to the "normal" reader who is not trained in modern theoretical physics, because in the views of the most modern theoretical physicists, "Physical Reality" transitions seamlessly into, *and includes*, what was traditionally called the "nonphysical realm." Reiterating, for reasons of simplicity, we distinguish between the physical and the nonphysical realms, while in reality there is no such difference.

   Accordingly, we can now distinguish between what is nonphysical and extraterrestrial. It is reasonable to assume that the laws of physics apply everywhere in the universe. Therefore, extraterrestrial life would still be subject to the laws of physics, even though it may contain and follow still unknown or undefined natural laws. *Nonphysical* would be distinctly different from *extraterrestrial* and much more similar to what is most commonly perceived as *spiritual*.

2. Of course, this statement excludes the steadily increasing number of people who have such unusual abilities as clairvoyance or possess the gift of mediumship. But these people are still a very small minority, and the vast majority of humans flat-out deny that these abilities exist and give them no credence.

3. Most digital cameras use *charge-coupled device* (CCD) sensors, while some higher-end cameras use *complementary metal oxide semiconductor* (CMOS) sensors. In both cases, the camera photo device (charge plate) consists of several million of tiny individual sensors (pixels), neatly arranged in a (hexagonal) closely packed array. Both sensor methods have distinct advantages and disadvantages. Important for orb photography is that high-quality CCD devices are more sensitive to capturing single photons than high-quality CMOS sensors. This is because each pixel on a CMOS sensor has several transistors located next to it, and many of the photons hitting the device hit the transistors instead of the photodiode and will thus not be detected. Therefore, CCD cameras—the vast majority of all digital cameras—are preferable, albeit not necessary, for orb photography. We have in our studies confirmed that a state-of-the-art Nikon D5000 CMOS-based camera does produce orbs but, as expected, in lesser quantities and with less definition (i.e., more "noise") of the interior of the orbs.

4. These points have been discussed in *The Orb Project* (Simon & Schuster, 2007), mostly in Klaus Heinemann's section.

5. While numerous researchers are studying "electronic voice perception" (EVP), which infringes on this topic, a clear correlation between orbs and EVP recordings has not yet been documented.

Chapter One: Authenticity of Orbs

1. William A. Tiller, Ph.D., *Psychoenergetic Science: A Second Copernican-Scale Revolution* (Walnut Creek, Calif.: Pavoir, 2007), www.tiller.org.

2. Mr. Vos's Website is www.dutchlightorbs.nl. He has hundreds, perhaps thousands, of photos with orbs taken with conventional photo cameras on commercial color emulsion film.

3. This argumentation is quite similar to a notion presented by Freddy Silva, a renowned researcher on crop circles, in a presentation given at the Prophets Conference on Orbs and Crop Circles (July 2008, Glastonbury, U.K). Discouraged by the relentless recurrence of skepticism regarding the authenticity of crop circles, and fueled by the circumstance that indeed some simple crop circles are proven to be man-made hoaxes, yet seeing the intricacy and sophistication of design of many authentic crop circles, Silva suggests that one should not get hung up with the question of authenticity. Instead, one should look beyond this at the *intricacy of design* of these crop circles, which may well have come about as primary thought implant, or inspiration, into those human beings who were, of course, totally oblivious to this happening and then fabricated the circles, rather than as primary conversion of that original thought into an unexplained physical

mechanism by which the crop circles were then made. Ultimately, Silva suggests, the "miracle" remains the same, and what we should be concerned with is finding out the real meaning behind it all.

4. It can be argued that it takes as few as about 1,000 photons of light to generate the image of an orb on a digital photograph in a CCD camera. The energy equivalent of 1,000 photons would be of the order of 1000EV or about 10^{-16} joule (approximately 10^{-17} calories; 10^{-19} BTU; 10^{-23} kilowatt-hours, or 10^{-16} watt-seconds). You would need about *one billion billion* times this amount of energy to keep an average (100-watt) lightbulb lit for just one second.

5. These are all assumptions discussed in *The Orb Project*.

Chapter Two: Orbs as Transforming Symbols

1. Leo Kim, Ph.D., molecular geneticist and CEO of a biotech firm, author of *Healing the Rift: Bridging the Gap Between Science and Spirituality*, keynote presentation at Science and Consciousness Conference, Santa Fe, N.M., 2009.

Chapter Three: Messages Based on Location

1. "A Life in the Day: Klaus Heinemann," Sunday *Times* (London), August 31, 2008.

Chapter Four: General Messages

1. In this presentation we primarily discussed material covered in *The Orb Project*.

Chapter Seven: Orbs at Epochal Events

1. Harry Rathbun, *Creative Initiative: Guide to Fulfillment* (Palo Alto, Calif.: Creative Initiative Foundation, 1976). Out of print.

Chapter Nine: Orbs at Home

1. Quotes are courtesy of Lisa and Amy Bradley.

Chapter Ten: Facial Features in Orbs

1. Quotes in this sub-chapter are courtesy of Freda Chaney, Mount Vernon, Ohio, February–November 2009.

2. Freda Chaney subsequently wrote *George Eliot Lives: An Incredible Story of Reincarnation,* about her experiences with this *Mill on the Floss* orb story.

3. *Orbs: The Veil Is Lifting,* DVD, produced/directed by Seth Mead, Hope Mead, and Randy Mead (Hillsboro, Ore.: Beyond Words Publishing, 2008). The DVD presents the opinions and findings in personal interviews of seven orb researchers, among them Klaus and Gundi Heinemann.

Chapter Twelve: Spiritual Healing

1. When we talk about third-dimensional and fourth-dimensional activities, we mean something entirely different than what one commonly understands in physics as 3-dimensional space and 4-dimensional space-time. In the language used by some spiritual teachers, the third-dimensional

level is equivalent to our physical space-time reality. Essentially all our human activities occur in the third-dimensional level. The fourth-dimensional realm is the spiritual reality. Everything that is mechanical, that can be calculated and manipulated, is third-dimensional. The Ten Commandments are third-dimensional, but the *attitude* of abiding by them for the love of God and our fellow human beings and the world is fourth-dimensional. Becoming a medical doctor is third-dimensional, but compassion is fourth-dimensional. Worrying about the correct hand positions in Reiki is third-dimensional, but caring about the well-being of the client is a fourth-dimensional pursuit.

2. This subject is addressed in detail in the afterword of *The Orb Project*.

3. From our extensive study of orb photographing we have concluded, among other findings, that:

    (i) Orbs as emanations from Spirit Beings have extremely high mobility. In fact, we have speculated that their *normal* velocities are many orders of magnitude greater than the speed of light and that their normal, usual state of being is one of movement rather than rest, as is the case for beings in our physical reality.

    (ii) Spirit emanations can rapidly expand and contract. It is, in fact, plausible that the mechanism itself of motion of orbs is based on expansion and contraction: expansion to such a size that the intended new location is now included within the sphere of presence of the expanded orb, followed by contraction with that precise location remaining in the sphere of presence. This could occur over vast distances, even intergalactic distances—there would be no spatial limit.

Since the *total* energy of an orb would likely remain approximately constant during an expansion/contraction sequence, regardless of the size or volume it happens to occupy, it's energy *density* would change greatly with expansion and contraction. The smaller the size, the higher is its energy density. It is thus conceivable that orbs can contract to diameters that are so small that the energy *density* they attain in the small volume they are then taking up is comparatively very high. If the volume contracts to extremely small sizes, such as to that of cells or even molecules or atoms, the energy density they can then obtain is plausibly more than enough to profoundly affect states of physical objects, such cellular structures—sufficient to break or induce chemical bonds, or even vaporize entire cells.

(iii) Spirits are highly intelligent. The evidence for this conclusion is overwhelming and needs no further explanation. It has been presented in numerous examples in this book and in *The Orb Project*. It is, in fact, not unreasonable to surmise that the intelligence of evolved Spirits greatly surpasses human intelligence. It has, for example, been argued that consciousness is manifest in the spiritual reality, where it moves at essentially infinite velocities and is not subject to decay—perhaps analogous to superconductivity in the physical reality—but will remain available to tap into at any point in time by any being that has the appropriate "antenna" to do so. From our physical (human) frame of reference, Spirits will be able to acquire information and knowledge of all varieties, including what to do to heal a physical ailment, with essentially infinite speed, and they will be able to act upon that information infinitely fast.

4. It is customary in science to present a hypothesis as a fact, without qualifiers and fine print like "may be," "could be thought of as," or "may be assumed to." The hypothesis is then subjected to testing. If it withstands all critical arguments, it becomes an accepted rule or process. Our hypothesis has, so far, withstood various tests, but it is not at a stage of general acceptability.

5. In some cases, however, actual pieces of tissue—at times even hundreds of cubic centimeters in size—are removed during a visible surgery. In this case, removal of this tissue most certainly constitutes a significant secondary reason for visible surgeries.

Chapter Thirteen: The O'Jack Phenomenon

1. The words *vibrations* and *vibrational frequencies* have very specific meanings in science, and these are sometimes incompatible with how they are used in the context of holistic/spiritual healing and/or New Age philosophy/spirituality. Often, the word *frequency* is used where *amplitude* would be the more correct term, culminating in an indiscriminate inference that "raising vibrational frequencies" would be desirable.

    Everything vibrates, and characteristic vibrational frequencies can in principle be ascribed to everything that exists, from the subatomic particles to living cells to entire organs. Whereby it is true that a cell (or group of cells) that is "ill" (i.e., damaged, malfunctioning) has different characteristic vibrational frequencies than a healthy one, this "wrong" set of frequencies can be lower or higher than that of the healthy cell, entirely dependent on the specific status of the cell. It is, therefore, incomplete to indiscriminately aspire to raising of vibrational frequencies, because there may be just as many situations where lowering the frequency may be what is beneficial. Frequency adjustment or harmonizing would be more appropriate terms to use.

The frequency of a wave is determined by structural circumstances, i.e., it increases or decreases with a structural change, such as a mutation of a cell. The amplitude is indicative of strength; it increases or decreases with power. Often, especially if entrainment of a "healthy vibration" is desired, the goal would be to increase the amplitude of the wave. Breathing techniques, such as used in Network Chiropractic, Quantum Touch healing, rebirthing, or similar holistic healing modalities are most likely beneficial because of an increased amplitude, rather than a changed frequency of the healer's energy field.

2. In a recent communication, Dr. Vafa Michael Mayaddat revealed to me that he has obtained a similar through-the-lens-cap photograph, but only at one singular occasion, many years ago. He did indicate that his state of mind was greatly different from normal at that occasion. He was a young student and amateur photographer, and he had just witnessed a presentation by Dr. William Tiller and Stanislav O'Jack at Stanford University, and a combination of intense desire to reproduce what he had heard and feelings of uneasiness about a personal situation led to him taking the photo, a color Kodak slide, in his dorm.

3. William A. Tiller, *Some Science Adventures with Real Magic* (Walnut Creek, Calif.: Pavior Publishing, 2005).

Chapter Fourteen: Expanded Perspective

1. Of course there are, and we have so pointed out, occurrences when Spirit Beings have reportedly spoken or written messages, but this was not available to be perceived by all people, but only by a few people with special gifts of perception; and therefore the argument of critics quickly prevailed.

2. This concept was explored in Klaus Heinemann's *Expanding Perception* (New York: Word Association Publishers, 2004).

Appendix B: On the Authenticity of Orbs

1. This evidence of an orb photographed under ISO 14644-1 Class 7 clean room conditions was provided by Drs. Ulrich Volz and Andreas Burkart, Konstanz, Germany (February 2009). Since the topic of proof of authenticity of orbs is not the subject of this book but, nevertheless, very important for the credibility of this subject at large, we are presenting this exciting experiment in the Appendix.

Acknowledgments

This book was inspired by numerous orb enthusiasts who had read *The Orb Project* and sent us their orb photos with relevant stories, including: Joe Alfieri, Cindy Andrews, Susan Anthony, Jenny Ayers, Sharon Bailey, Amanda Bayer, Claudia Birk, Carol Boyette, Lisa Bradley, Berry Ann Brown, Karin Budni, Freda Chaney, Michelle Choquet, Marcia Cochenauer, Susan Cothern, Bob Ding and Diane Rose, Janice Driver, Dana Dureya, Toni Felice, Tamra Fleming, Lee Foster, Aimee Freeman, Larry Fulton, Adriana Galvez, Marie-Annick Glon, Horst Gruenfelder, Doug Hackett, Wayne Harman, Annabel Heinemann, Deidre Heppell, Sherri Herrmann, Andrew van Hoffelen, Linda Horton, Linda Moulton Howe, Flicka Johnson, Gary Jones, Iris Kaufmann, Charlie and Jann Kiesel, Hanna Kluner, Herb Lebherz, Rhonda Leslie, Coral Leybourne, Kay Marie Lobo, Connie and Rob Maday, Ursula Maeder, Camila Martinez, Beverley Massey, Claire Mataira, Colleen May, Laura McClellan, Malcolm McLean, Hope Mead, Negin Minaee, Kay McCue, Dominick Nicolotti, Barbara Ostby, Darren Owen, Elke Paul, Frank Peters, Renee Pisarz, Grazyna Prykiel, Wes Rockie, Rhea Sampson, Sandra Sanders, Peter Schur, Elizabeth Severino, Vanessa Shuba, Christine Sigg, Charles Spangler, Goran Spasowski, Marcin Stasewski, Renate Strang, Susan Strine, Carol Thornton, Sandra Underwood, Ulrich Volz, Ed Vos, Margaret Weber, Manuel Weihrauch,

Elizabeth Whitfield, Alan Whitley, Diane Wipperfurt, Grace Wu, and Zane and Julia Zane. Although we could only include a small fraction of these stories in this book, they are all valuable and reinforced and confirmed those that we selected.

Special thanks are due to Dana Dureya and Elke Paul for sharing their insights after reading an early draft of the manuscript. Virginia Essene and Freda Chaney independently thoroughly reviewed the manuscript. We thank them for numerous valuable suggestions along the way.

We also give our heartfelt thanks to Medium João Teixeira de Faria for encouragement in the publication process. We appreciate Hazel Courteney's initiative for leading us to her book agent, Susan Mears, who enthusiastically found several potential publishers, among whom we selected Hay House, who had for years impressed us as publisher of numerous choice books. We were very impressed with the expertise, dedication, and timeliness of the Hay House editing staff, in particular Laura Koch and Melanie Gold, without whom the ambitious publication timeline could not have been met.

Most of all, we thank the Beings from beyond who have contributed to the pictures and their interpretations in this book.

About the Authors

Klaus Heinemann was born and educated in Germany and holds a Ph.D. in experimental physics from the University of Tübingen. Dr. Heinemann worked for many years in materials science research at NASA and UCLA, and as research professor at Stanford University. He also worked in solar energy engineering and ozone water purification and holds several patents in these areas.

Gundi Heinemann studied education in Germany and teaches numerous alternative medicine disciplines. She runs a wellness coaching/healing arts practice in California.

They have been married for over 40 years and reside in the San Francisco Bay Area. They can be contacted via www.theHeinemanns.net.

Hay House Titles of Related Interest

YOU CAN HEAL YOUR LIFE, the movie,
starring Louise L. Hay & Friends
(available as a 1-DVD program
and an expanded 2-DVD set)
Watch the trailer at: **www.LouiseHayMovie.com**

THE SHIFT, the movie,
starring Dr. Wayne W. Dyer
(available as a 1-DVD program
and an expanded 2-DVD set)
Watch the trailer at: **www.DyerMovie.com**

O

MESSAGES FROM WATER AND THE UNIVERSE,
by Masaru Emoto

THE SPONTANEOUS HEALING OF BELIEF:
Shattering the Paradigm of False Limits,
by Gregg Braden

THE VORTEX: Where the Law of Attraction
Assembles All Cooperative Relationships,
by Esther and Jerry Hicks (The Teachings of Abraham®)

All of the above are available at your local bookstore,
or may be ordered by contacting Hay House (see next page).

O

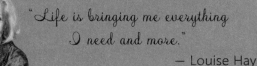